Country Walks Near
C H I C A G O

by
Alan Fisher

RAMBLER BOOKS

Baltimore 1987

COUNTRY WALKS NEAR CHICAGO

by Alan Fisher
Maps and photographs by the author

Rambler Books
1430 Park Avenue
Baltimore, MD 21217

Copyright © 1987 by Alan Hall Fisher

If you notice errors in the text or maps, please point them out in a letter to the publisher.

Printed in the United States of America.

FIRST EDITION

ISBN 0-9614963-1-2

10 9 8 7 6 5 4 3 2 1

CONTENTS

Preface   10

1   **Illinois Beach State Park**   12
*Walking or ski touring — 4 miles (6.4 kilometers).
A footpath follows the bank of the Dead River to
the Lake Michigan shore. From the mouth of the
river, walk north along the beach, then return
through prairie and scrubby woods.*

2   **Edward L. Ryerson Conservation Area**   20
*Walking or ski touring — 1 or more miles (1.6 or
more kilometers). A network of trails explores
farm fields, meadows, and deep woods along
the Des Plaines River.*

3   **Chicago Botanic Garden**   26
*Walking — 1 or more miles (1.6 or more
kilometers). A wide variety of specialty gardens
display native and exotic plants, all attractively
arranged on several islands in the Skokie
Lagoons.*

4   **Des Plaines River Trail**   32
*Walking or ski touring — up to 8 or 10 miles
(12.9 or 16.1 kilometers) roundtrip. Several short
trails (each less than a mile) are located at the
River Trail Nature Center, and the River Trail itself
stretches downstream 4 miles and upstream 5
miles along the east bank of the Des Plaines
River.*

5   Waterfall Glen Forest Preserve   **46**
*Walking or ski touring — 9 miles (14.5
kilometers). The trail circles through rolling
terrain, occasionally passing ponds, marshes,
and steep ravines. Woods alternate with prairie
and overgrown fields.*

6   Palos Hills Forest Preserve   **54**
northeast section
*Walking or ski touring — 5.5 miles (8.9
kilometers). Starting at the Little Red
Schoolhouse Nature Center, follow a bridle path
through woods dotted with meadows, marshes,
and ponds. Several shorter footpaths also start
from the nature center.*

7   Palos Hills Forest Preserve   **68**
southern section
*Walking or ski touring — 4 miles (6.4 kilometers).
The trail explores the bluff and wooded
highlands that overlook the Sag Channel,
through which lake Michigan once drained to
the southwest.*

8   Indiana Dunes State Park   **76**
*Walking or ski touring — 5 miles (8 kilometers).
Sand ridges rise nearly two hundred feet from
the southern shore of Lake Michigan. Cross the
high foredunes and follow the beach to the Big
Blowout, then return through sheltered woods
behind the dunes.*

9   Indiana Dunes National Lakeshore   **90**
West Beach
Walking or ski touring — 5 miles (8 kilometers).

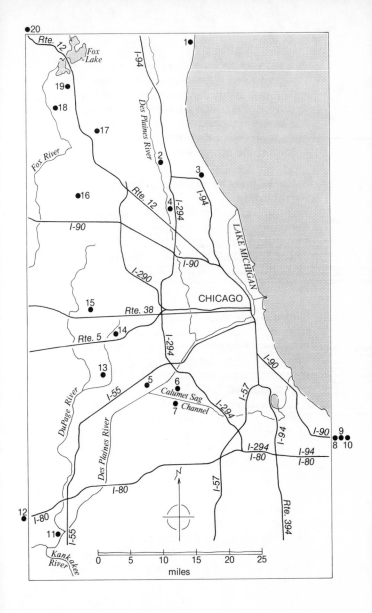

In a series of segments, this excursion passes through several different dune environments. After a walk along the beach, cross the high foredunes, then circle the flats where the sand has been strip mined. From a ridge overlooking Long Lake, return through the wooded hills and hollows of the backdunes.

**10   Indiana Dunes National Lakeshore   104
        Mount Baldy**
        *Walking — up to 4 miles (6.4 kilometers),
        depending on the condition of the beach west of
        Mount Baldy. Explore the Saharan plateau atop
        Mount Baldy, then follow the narrow beach
        along the base of the bluff. Return by the way
        you came.*

11   Illinois and Michigan Canal   112
        *Walking, bicycling, and ski touring — up to 15
        miles (24.2 kilometers) one way. Hike from
        Channahon to Morris (or vice versa) along one
        of the most attractive sections of this historic
        commercial waterway. For 5 miles along the
        Kankakee Bluffs, the towpath overlooks the Des
        Plaines and Illinois Rivers, then cuts through
        woods and fields before again bordering the
        Illinois River at Morris. Several access points are
        described, making possible a series of shorter
        trips.*

12   Starved Rock State Park   126
        *Walking — 4.5 miles (7.2 kilometers). Rock
        pinnacles, cliffs, and canyons border the Illinois
        River at Starved Rock State Park. From Starved
        Rock itself, follow the river upstream past Eagle*

Cliff to LaSalle Canyon. Return along the rim of the bluffs.

13   Greene Valley Forest Preserve   **134**
*Walking or ski touring — 5 miles (8 kilometers).
Passing through meadows, overgrown fields,
scrubby woods, and mature forest, the trail links
upland and flood plain along the East Branch of
the DuPage River.*

14   Morton Arboretum   **140**
*Walking — 2 to 4 miles (3.2 to 6.4 kilometers),
depending on which of several trail loops you
follow. The arboretum features groves of
specimen trees and shrubs, as well as gardens,
meadows, and native woods — all
interconnected by an extensive trail network.*

15   Illinois Prairie Path   **150**
**   Wheaton to Elgin**
*Walking, bicycling, or ski touring — up to 14
miles (22.5 kilometers) one way. Walk from
Wheaton to the outskirts of Elgin (or vice versa)
along an old railroad that now forms a hiker's
highway through woods, fields, and marsh.*

16   Crabtree Nature Center   **160**
*Walking — 3 miles (4.8 kilometers). The chief
attraction here is variety: farm fields, orchard,
meadow, woods, prairie, marshes, and ponds.*

17   Lakewood Forest Preserve   **168**
*Walking or ski touring — 1 or more miles (1.6 or
more kilometers). A network of trails explores a
rolling landscape of forest, fields, ponds, and
marsh.*

18   Moraine Hills State Park   **178**
*Walking, bicycling, or ski touring — 3.5 or 7
miles (5.6 or 11.3 kilometers), depending on
whether you take one loop or two. The trails
meander through an intriguing landscape of
knolls, ridges, marshes, and lakes, seemingly
distributed without rhyme or reason.*

19   Volo Bog   **188**
*Walking — 0.5 mile (0.8 kilometer). A floating
boardwalk penetrates to the center of the bog,
passing through zones of tamarack, leatherleaf,
sphagnum moss, and other unusual plants.*

20   Kettle Moraine State Forest   **196**
**   southern unit**
*Walking or ski touring — 2 to 9 miles (3.2 to 14.5
kilometers), depending on which of several trail
circuits you follow. The trails climb, dip, and
wind through a remarkable landscape of
irregular hills and abrupt depressions.*

**   Bibliography**   **204**

PREFACE

THERE'S STILL TIME for a walk in the woods, even if you've spent all morning working or sleeping late.

This book is for people who want an outing in the country without wasting half the day getting there and coming back. If you live in the Chicago region, the excursions described here are close at hand. The walks have been planned to show the best parts of Chicago's countryside and to encourage everyone to use the many parks, forest preserves, and trails maintained by federal, state, and county agencies and private conservation groups. Each chapter of this book includes a brief introduction, a map, directions, and commentary on the area's natural or social history. The routes cover the gamut of local landscapes: woods, prairies, farms, glacial moraines, ponds, marsh, river valleys, lakeshore, and duneland. All the areas included here are open to the public, and many are excellent for ski touring as well as walking.

A few comments on how to dress and what to bring. Wear shoes that you do not mind getting muddy or wet. Sneakers or running shoes are adequate in warm weather; hiking boots are advisable during winter. I usually carry a small knapsack containing a sandwich, a plastic water bottle, perhaps a sweater or rain parka, and some insect repellent during summer. I also recommend binoculars, which in recent years have become quite inexpensive, and will add endlessly to your enjoyment.

It is customary in books such as this to include a catalog of cautions about poison ivy, slippery rocks, and the like. Such a list follows, but more generally, of course, what is needed is simply common sense. Thousands of people yearly walk the trails described here without injury, but there are always those who are hurt or even killed because they fail to take ordinary care or willfully take extraordinary risks. Specifically, during winter do not walk on frozen rivers, ponds, or lakes. Do not go swimming except where and when permitted. Where the routes follow roads for short distances, walk well off the road on the shoulder to minimize the risk of being hit by a car, and use caution, especially at dusk or after dark, where the routes cross roads and railroads. (Studies show that in poor light conditions, motorists typically cannot even see pedestrians in time to stop, so your safety depends entirely on you.) In sum, use good judgment and common sense to evaluate the particular circumstances that you find, and do not undertake any unusual risks.

It is anticipated that for each of the areas described here, readers will be coming from different directions; accordingly, the instructions sometimes include alternative avenues of approach. Read through the automobile directions before you start in order to pinpoint your destination and to pick the best way to get there. You may also find it useful to have the *Chicago Tribune's* Chicagoland Map, which on one side or the other shows all the areas featured in this book.

I have received information or other help for this book from the following people: Nan Buckardt, Rebecca Goldberg, and Steve E. Meyer, all of the Ryerson Conservation Area, Andrew S. Kimmel of the Forest Preserve District of DuPage County, Susan Serritella of the DuPage County Highway Department, and Elaine B. Tredinnick of the Friends of Volo Bog. Very many thanks also to my father's sister and brother, Margaret Fisher and Walter T. Fisher, for their interest in and help with this project. I also want to mention my grandfather, Walter L. Fisher, whom I never knew because I was born after his death, but whose interest in the out-of-doors and in conservation was passed on to his children and has much to do with this book.

A.F.

1

ILLINOIS BEACH STATE PARK

Walking or ski touring — 4 miles (6.4 kilometers). A footpath follows the bank of the Dead River to the Lake Michigan shore. From the mouth of the river, walk north along the beach, then return through prairie and scrubby woods. During winter, do not walk on the shelf of ice that sometimes extends out from the shore over the water. Dogs are prohibited. Open daily from dawn until dusk. Managed by the Illinois Department of Conservation. Telephone (312) 662-4811 or 662-4828.

AERIAL PHOTOGRAPHS of Illinois Beach State Park show a series of parallel ridges and troughs like oversized corrugations of a plowed field. The ridges and furrows follow the trend of the lakeshore, but they curve slightly inland toward the southern end of the park, as indicated by the stippled ridge outlines shown on the map. (To avoid congesting the map, the ridges are not shown north of the Dead River, but they are there in reality.) Because the difference in elevation between the dry ridges and moist troughs is slight, the shift from one to the other is sometimes defined only be subtle changes in vegetation. The hairpin turns of the Dead River also reflect the ridge-and-trough topography. Some of the larger ridges are easily discernible along the walk outlined at the end of this chapter, and if you take the extra time to obtain a permit and access directions from the park office, you can also explore the restricted area south of the Dead River, where the ridge complex is most clearly developed.

What accounts for this peculiar terrain, with a surface like a washboard? The ridge nearest the lake is a feature familiar to everyone: it is simply a foredune made of sand blown inland from the beach and anchored by marram grass, cottonwood, and other dune plants. All the other ridges are the same feature repeated many times: a series of ancient foredunes, now arrayed in ranks one behind the other. Each ridge marks the location of the lakefront at a different time during the last two thousand years or so, when the level of the lake appears to have fluctuated by as much as six feet above and below the present level because of variations in climate. Over many hundreds of years, sand that was eroded from the lakeshore north of the park has been washed southward by the longshore current and deposited here. As the sand accumulated, the beach grew wider, leading to the development of new foredunes in front of the old. The result is a broad expanse of sand ridges extending into what was once the lake. From the shoreline, the body of sand continues east as an underwater apron stretching offshore several thousand feet.

Aside from the ranks of ancient foredunes, other evidence supports the view that the lakeshore in the vicinity of Illinois Beach State Park has been moving eastward as sand has accumulated. About a mile inland from the present shoreline is a clay bluff such as borders the lake farther south in Lake Bluff, Lake Forest, Highland Park, Glencoe, and Winnetka. Almost certainly the lake once lapped against the foot of this bluff in the vicinity of Waukegan. Also, borings at the state park show an underlying layer of very fine sand such as accumulates in an offshore environment. On top of the fine sand is another layer of coarse sand and gravel, such as accumulates in a nearshore environment. Taken together, the bore samples suggest that what is now dry land was once located a short distance from shore, and that earlier still the area was far offshore.

The most direct evidence that the "beach ridge complex" (as geologists call the entire formation) has been spreading eastward is provided by marine surveys conducted within the last

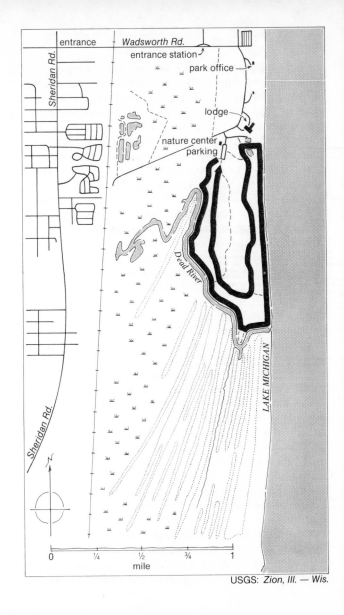

entrance Wadsworth Rd.
entrance station
park office
Sheridan Rd.
lodge
nature center
parking
Dead River
LAKE MICHIGAN
Sheridan Rd.

N

0   ¼   ½   ¾   1
mile

USGS: *Zion, Ill. — Wis.*

15

one hundred years. The shoreline and underwater topography in the area of Illinois Beach State Park were charted in 1872-1873 by the U.S. Lake Survey. The area was charted again in 1950-1955 by the Illinois Division of Waterways. A comparison of the two surveys shows that during the eighty-year interval, the land at the southern end of Illinois Beach State Park advanced into the lake about one thousand feet and that a blanket of sand about ten feet thick was added to the lake bottom near the shore. In the vicinity of the park lodge, however, and for a distance of about two miles to the north and two miles to the south of the lodge, the shoreline remained more or less static. And to the north, in the vicinity of the Wisconsin-Illinois boundary, the shore receded westward about seven hundred feet and the lake bottom became deeper. This is the area from which sand has been removed by erosion and swept southward by the longshore current to build the beach ridge complex seen today at Illinois Beach State Park. In contrast to the broad expanse of sand ridges and the smooth shoreline at the state beach, the shoreline farther north is very irregular, with little or no beach in most areas, and a number of promentories that extend into the lake. These projections are actually homesites protected by riprap to retard the erosion that already has eaten away at the neighboring shoreline.

The process of erosion in the north and deposition in the south suggests that the entire beach ridge complex — a body of sand about 9 miles long and .75 to 1.1 miles wide — is slowly migrating southward. Soil profiles and peat samples dated by radiocarbon methods demonstrate that the oldest beach sediments are located in the northwestern corner of the area and that the sediments become younger to the south and east. This pattern matches what would be expected if the entire beach ridge complex were moving south as erosion gnaws away at the northern flank and transports sand to the southern flank. In all likelihood, shoreline that currently is undergoing accretion (as at the southern end of the state park) soon will shift to a period of equilibrium followed by gradual and steady loss (as already is occurring in the northern half of the state park). The same processes that constructed rank upon rank of low sand ridges at the state park will, in time, partially or completely devour them.

AUTOMOBILE: Illinois Beach State Park is located a few miles north of Waukegan. The entrance is on Sheridan Road at a crossroads with Wadsworth Road.

From downtown Chicago take Interstate 90 (Kennedy Expressway) northwest, then switch to Interstate 94 (Edens Expressway) toward Milwaukee. At Exit 29 (the next exit after Dundee Road) follow I-94 west to join the Tri-State Tollway toward Milwaukee. The Tri-State Tollway northbound can also be joined as it passes west of Chicago.

Follow the Tri-State Tollway north to the exit for Route 132 (Grand Avenue) east toward Waukegan. (Ignore the highway sign saying that traffic for Illinois Beach State Park should take Rosecrans Road, which involves another toll and longer mileage without significant advantage.)

From the top of the exit ramp off the tollway, follow Route 132 east 3.2 miles, then turn left onto Route 131 (Green Bay Road). Go 4.1 miles, then turn right onto Wadsworth Road. Follow Wadsworth Road 3.5 miles to the entrance for Illinois Beach State Park.

From the entrance station at Illinois Beach State Park, continue to a four-way intersection. Turn right and go 0.5 mile, then turn left toward the nature center. Veer right immediately into the parking lot.

From the suburbs north of Chicago, Route 41 (the northward extension of Edens Expressway) also provides a convenient approach to Route 132 and Illinois Beach State Park. If you go via Route 41, note that the exit at Route 132 is from the left lane. Turn right at the bottom of the exit ramp and go 0.7 mile to Green Bay Road. Turn left and follow Green Bay Road 4.1 miles, then turn right

and follow Wadsworth Road 3.5 miles to the park entrance. From there, follow the directions in the preceding paragraph.

WALK: From the southwest corner of the parking lot (that is, on the same side as the nature center building, but at the other end of the lot), follow the Dead River Trail through sparse, scrubby woods and along the marsh next to the Dead River. Pass a trail intersecting from the left; continue along the river's edge. Eventually, follow the path as it cuts left across a point of land, then rejoins the river's edge. Continue to the shore of Lake Michigan.

At the lakefront, turn left. With the lake on the right, follow the beach north about 1 mile. When you come abreast of some corrugated steel piles and shoring before reaching the lodge (or beach hotel), turn inland. Join a path located about 20 yards north of the end of the steel shoring. Follow the path inland about 200 yards along the crest of a sandy dike between two ponds. At a road paved with gravel, sand, and grass, turn left. Follow the road clockwise in a circuit through scrub, dunes, and forest back to the parking lot. (Or, to return more directly to the parking lot, follow the road only 360 yards, then turn right onto a sandy path marked with stakes; this path leads directly to the parking lot.)

2

EDWARD L. RYERSON CONSERVATION AREA

Walking or ski touring — 1 or more miles (1.6 or more kilometers). A network of trails explores farm fields, meadows, and deep woods along the Des Plaines River. Dogs are prohibited. Open daily 9:00 A.M. to 5:00 P.M. during March through October; open 8:30 A.M. to 4:30 P.M. during November through February. Managed by the Lake County Forest Preserve District. Telephone (312) 948-7750.

THE RYERSON CONSERVATION AREA is outstanding not only for what it is — a large tract of mature bottomland forest and farmland bordering the Des Plaines River — but also for how it came to be. This property, so valuable from an aesthetic and environmental perspective, obviously also has great worth in terms of its potential for residential development, yet most of the land was given to Lake County in the late 1960s by owners who had grown to love the area as it was and who wished to see it preserved in a natural state.

The result might easily have been very different. In the mid-1920s, the land that now forms the southern part of the Ryerson Area was acquired by a group of investors interested in land speculation. Their plan was to sell their entire holding of several hundred acres to subdividers. Among the first sales, however, were some parcels of fifteen acres purchased by individuals who had no immediate plans for development and who, in at least one or two cases, were simply seeking weekend retreats. The idea caught on, and instead of subdividing their

property into house lots, the owners saved large parcels for their own recreational use and sold the rest to a few like-minded buyers. Although most built cabins, none of the owners at first thought of anything but eventual sale to subdividers for conventional housing.

At about the same time, Edward and Nora Ryerson acquired land nearby, and in 1928 they built a small log cabin on the banks of the Des Plaines River. In 1939 the Ryersons purchased a large tract to the north of their cabin from an elderly resident of the area named Whigham, who was a descendant of Daniel Wright, said to be the first settler in Lake County. After the Ryersons acquired the Whigham property, they built the farm buildings seen today and hired a farmer to run the operation, which they called Brushwood Farm. Later the Ryersons built a handsome house (finished in 1942 and now the education center), using old, weathered bricks and other material salvaged from the demolition of a woolen mill in Hanover, Illinois. After completion of the house, the Ryersons made Brushwood Farm their home for the remainder of their lives.

During the 1950s and '60s, the area remained essentially unchanged, even as suburban development in the region accelerated after World War II. Eventually, Mr. Ryerson and some of the neighboring landowners began to talk informally among themselves about the future of their land and the possibility of preserving it in a natural state by giving or selling it to the Lake County Forest Preserve District, which Mr. Ryerson had helped to form in 1958. The large Ryerson property was plainly necessary to the project, and so as years passed the other owners looked to the Ryersons to take the first step. This the Ryersons did starting in 1966, when they sold eighty-five acres to the Lake County Forest Preserve District and established a schedule to give, both during their lives and by bequest, the rest of their land to the county.

During the following three years, several neighboring landowners also gave their land to the county, and others proved to be willing to sell, in some cases at prices substantially below

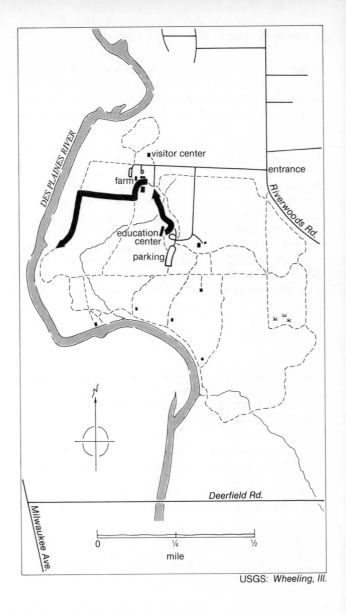

DES PLAINES RIVER

visitor center

entrance

farm

Riverwoods Rd.

education center

parking

Deerfield Rd.

Milwaukee Ave.

0   ¼   ½

mile

USGS: *Wheeling, Ill.*

23

market value. In this manner, without there ever having been any group action or formal arrangement among the Ryersons and the smaller owners, the county eventually acquired a preserve that presently totals 550 acres. Of this the Ryersons gave more than half, and the rest came from Mr. and Mrs. Ivan Albright, Mr. and Mrs. Rosecrans Baldwin, Mr. Edward Barnes, Mr. and Mrs. Chauncy Borland, Mr. David Dangler, Mr. and Mrs. Walter T. Fisher, Dr. and Mrs. John S. Garvin, Mr. Henry Preston, Dr. and Mrs. John Schweppe, and Mr. and Mrs. Hermon D. Smith. All were glad to have the preserve carry the name of the major benefactor: Edward L. Ryerson.

After you have visited the Ryerson Conservation Area, you may want to consider joining the Friends of Ryerson Woods, a group whose modest annual membership fee helps to support various activities held at the conservation area. Members receive a newsletter of activities and discounts on programs and materials. For information write to the Friends of Ryerson Woods, Edward L. Ryerson Conservation Area, 21950 Riverwoods Road, Deerfield, Illinois 60015, or telephone (312) 948-7750.

AUTOMOBILE: The Ryerson Conservation Area is located north of Chicago in Riverwoods. The entrance is on Riverwoods Road 1.7 miles north of the intersection with Deerfield Road.

From downtown Chicago take Interstate 90 (Kennedy Expressway) northwest, then switch to Interstate 94 (Edens Expressway) toward Milwaukee. At Exit 29 (the next exit after Dundee Road) follow I-94 west to join the Tri-State Tollway toward Milwaukee. Leave the tollway at Deerfield Road, which is the first exit after the Deerfield Road Toll Plaza. (Presently, there is only one exit ramp at Deerfield Road, but if a full cloverleaf is developed, take the westbound exit.) The Deerfield Road exit can also be reached by joining the Tri-State Tollway northbound as it passes west of Chicago.

RYERSON CONSERVATION AREA

From the top of the exit ramp off the tollway at Deerfield Road, turn left (or, if a westbound exit has been built, merge smoothly onto Deerfield Road). Go 0.5 mile west on Deerfield Road, then turn right onto Riverwoods Road. Follow Riverwoods Road 1.7 miles, then turn left into the Edward L. Ryerson Conservation Area. Follow the entrance drive for 0.2 mile, then turn left toward the main parking lot.

If you are driving from somewhere in Lake County, go directly to Deerfield Road, which connects Milwaukee Road and Waukegan Road a mile north of the boundary between Lake County and Cook County. At the intersection of Deerfield Road and Riverwoods Road 0.5 mile west of the Tri-State Tollway, turn north and go 1.7 miles to the Edward L. Ryerson Conservation Area on the left.

WALK: After stopping by the education center and library in the Ryerson house, turn left out the front door and follow a path and road to the farm visible a few hundred yards away. A visitor center is located in a log structure just north of the farm complex.

At the farm, join a gravel drive as it curves left behind the barn. At the corner of a fenced field on the right, turn right and follow a grassy path along the edge of the field; with a fence on the left, go straight to the far end of the field. Turn left at a T-intersection, and from there continue on a circuit along the riverside trail or any of the other paths.

3

CHICAGO BOTANIC GARDEN

Walking — 1 or more miles (1.6 or more kilometers). A wide variety of specialty gardens display native and exotic plants, all attractively arranged on several islands in the Skokie Lagoons. Dogs are prohibited. An admission fee is charged. Open daily (except Christmas) 8:00 A.M. until sunset. Managed by the Chicago Horticultural Society. Telephone (312) 835-5440.

SCIENTIFIC BOTANIC GARDENS are an outgrowth of the work of renaissance herbalists — that is, men who wrote books (called herbals) containing descriptions and illustrations of herbs and other plants, together with discussions of their various "virtues" that made them useful as medicines. Most herbals were written between the late 1400s and late 1600s, and they contained a blend of painstakingly accurate observation and fantastic superstition, including, for example, the "doctrine of signatures" by which a plant's medicinal powers were based on the superficial resemblance of certain plant parts to specific human organs. Thus various heart-shaped leaves were thought to relieve heart disease, and the walnut, which has a shell with a convoluted surface like the cerebral cortex, was prescribed for brain disease.

The herbalists and their herbals stimulated the founding of botanic gardens or "physic gardens" in association with early medical schools at various universities. For example, the circular design of the Heritage Garden at the Chicago Botanic Garden is based on Europe's first scientific botanic garden,

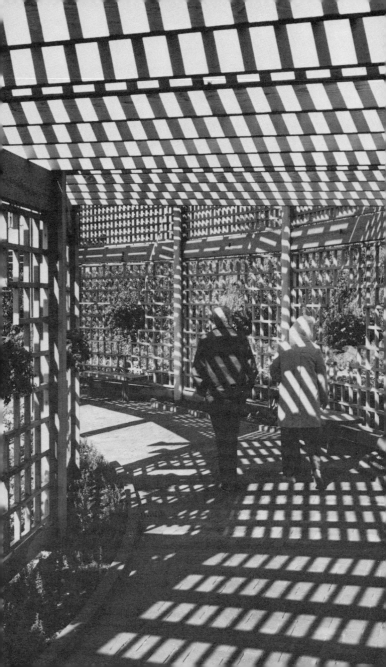

started in 1545 at the University of Padua in Italy. Professors of medicine were the principal botanists of that time, and their physic gardens provided training for students as well as a source of plants for medicines. At the end of the sixteenth century, there were five such gardens in Europe; two centuries later, there were 1,600 botanic gardens. The botanists of the seventeenth century, however, turned away from medical botany and instead sought to describe all plants, including the many new ones that were being introduced to Europe in large numbers from Asia, Africa, and America by explorers and settlers. Botanic gardens affiliated with medical schools declined and were replaced by gardens devoted mainly to plant collecting, to research in plant culture, and to the display of ornamental and exotic plants, as at England's Royal Botanic Gardens at Kew and now at the Chicago Botanic Garden.

The circular heritage Garden at the Chicago Botanic Garden is also a memorial to Carolus Linnaeus, and a large statue said to represent Linnaeus dominates one quadrant of the circle. Linnaeus was a Swedish botanist and taxonomist (or classifier) who lived from 1707 to 1778. He was the first to form principles for defining genera and species of plants and other organisms and to create a uniform system for naming them. In 1753 he published *Species Plantarum,* which contains careful descriptions of six thousand species of plants from all parts of the world known at that time. In this work, Linnaeus established the practice of binomial nomenclature — that is, the denomination of each kind of plant by two words, the genus name and the species name, as in *Acer rubrum,* or red maple. Binomial nomenclature had been introduced much earlier by some of the herbalists, but it was not generally accepted until Linnaeus devised a comprehensive taxonomic methodology.

The Heritage Garden itself is organized according to Linnaeus' system of plant classification. But before discussing the basis for that system, here is a question: How would you, if confronted with the task of classifying and cataloguing the hundreds of thousands of varieties of known plants, go about

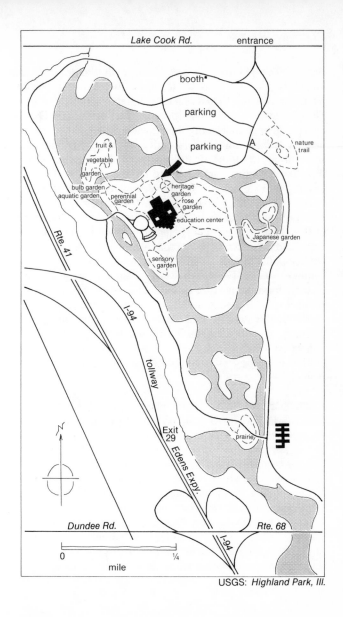

Lake Cook Rd.   entrance

booth

parking

parking

A   nature trail

fruit & vegetable garden

bulb garden
aquatic garden

perennial garden

heritage garden
rose garden

education center

Japanese garden

sensory garden

Rte. 41

I-94

tollway

Exit 29

Edens Expy.

prairie

N

Dundee Rd.   Rte. 68

I-94

0   ¼
mile

USGS: *Highland Park, Ill.*

29

the job? Theophrastus, a Greek botanist who studied with Plato and Aristotle and who wrote about two hundred botanical treatises, classified plants merely as trees, shrubs, and herbs. Dioscorides, a Greek botanist of the first century, A.D., also grouped plants under only three headings: aromatic, culinary, and medicinal. Until the invention of the compound microscope about 1590, the identification and classification of plants were for the most part based on large features such as size, shape, and external structure of leaves, roots, and stems.

And what was the basis of Linnaeus' system? He referred mainly to plants' sexual characteristics, by which the number of flower parts — especially stamens, which produce male sex cells, and styles, which are prolongations of plant ovaries that receive pollen grains — serve as useful tools for easy identification of plants. For non-flowering plants, other reproductive features form the basis of classification. Although artificial, as Linnaeus himself acknowledged, such a system has the great merit of facilitating the rapid placement of a plant into a named category, and this approach still dominates plant taxonomy today despite the advent of more modern systems based on new evidence about natural evolutionary relationships among plants.

AUTOMOBILE: The Chicago Botanic Garden is located north of Chicago in Glencoe. The entrance is on Lake Cook Road 0.6 mile east of Edens Expressway.

From downtown Chicago take Interstate 90 (Kennedy Expressway) northwest, then switch to Interstate 94 (Edens Expressway) toward Milwaukee. Where I-94 heads west at Exit 29 (the next exit after Dundee Road), continue straight north on Route 41 toward Waukegan. Leave Route 41 at Lake Cook Road. From the top of the exit ramp, turn right. Follow Lake Cook Road east 0.6 mile, then turn right into the Chicago Botanic Garden. From the entrance booth, follow the drive to the parking lots on the left.

WALK: Go first to the centrally located education center and the adjacent demonstration gardens.

If, after wandering through the various gardens near the education center, you want a longer walk, go to the crossroads (marked A on the map) east of the parking lots. Follow the circumferential road toward the exit at Dundee Road. After 20 yards, you will reach the entrance to a short nature trail on the left. Or you can continue along the road shoulder for 0.7 mile to a road intersecting from a bridge on the right. Turn right across the bridge. Only 10 yards after crossing the bridge, turn right into the Prairie area. From here you can continue around the circumferential road or return to the parking lots by the way you came.

4

DES PLAINES RIVER TRAIL

Walking or ski touring — up to 8 or 10 miles (12.9 or 16.1 kilometers) roundtrip. Several short trails (each less than a mile) are located at the River Trail Nature Center, and the River Trail itself stretches downstream 4 miles and upstream 5 miles along the east bank of the Des Plaines River. Downstream the trail passes through forest and fields; upstream the route is almost wholly wooded. If you do not want to retrace your steps, a car shuttle is necessary. The parking lot and short trails at the nature center are open daily (except Thanksgiving, Christmas, and New Year's Day) 8:00 A.M. to 5:00 P.M. during summer and 8:00 A.M. to 4:00 P.M. during winter. Dogs are prohibited at the nature center. The River Trail itself is open daily from dawn until dusk. If you plan to use the River Trail early in the morning or late in the afternoon, park your car in the Allison Woods lot off Milwaukee Avenue just north of the nature center, as shown on Map 1. Managed by the Forest Preserve District of Cook County. Telephone (312) 261-8400 from the city or 366-9420 from the suburbs.

THE DES PLAINES RIVER rises in southeastern Wisconsin and flows south toward Chicago in a course parallel with the Lake Michigan shore. Ten miles due west of the Loop, the elevation of the river is about twenty-five feet higher than the lake, but the Des Plaines never enters Lake Michigan because the way is barred by a low ridge (reflected in such place names as Park Ridge, Harwood Heights, and Norridge) that is part of the system of glacial moraines that border the lake.

From the suburbs west of Chicago, the Des Plaines River turns southwest. Its confluence with the Kankakee River below Joliet forms the Illinois River, which ultimately joins the Mississippi River. During the early days of European exploration and fur trading, the proximity of the Chicago River (with its mouth at Lake Michigan) and the Des Plaines River provided an easy portage that made the mouth of the Chicago River an advantageous site for the trading post and settlement that eventually grew into the nation's largest inland city.

If by now you have taken some of the walks outlined in this book, you probably have noticed that there is more variety to our local landscape than the region commonly is given credit for. One major variable is the extent to which the different areas that are featured here have been affected by our larger rivers, such as the Des Plaines, Fox, and DuPage. As is typical in regions across which continental glaciers have advanced and retreated, there are large areas near Chicago where there are no rivers or streams to speak of because a blanket of clay, sand, pebbles, and cobbles deposited by the glaciers has covered and, in large part, eradicated the old drainage systems. Now many small swales, gullies, and minor creeks that are dry or nearly dry between rainfalls carry stormwater runoff to myriad lakes, ponds, and marshes that have no discernible outlet or interconnection, as at Crabtree Nature Center, Lakewood Forest Preserve, and countless other places, especially in northwestern Cook County and in Lake County, so-named because of its numerous small lakes. These areas of low, rolling hills and confused surface drainage are the region's upland, as yet showing only rudimentary stream development.

Other areas show more advanced stream development. At Greene Valley, for example, the upland slopes down to a wide flood plain carved by the East Branch of the DuPage River. And at Waterfall Glen, small, continuously-flowing streams (such as Sawmill Creek) have incised ravines that penetrate to bedrock; these small streams drain into the Des Plaines River,

MAP 1

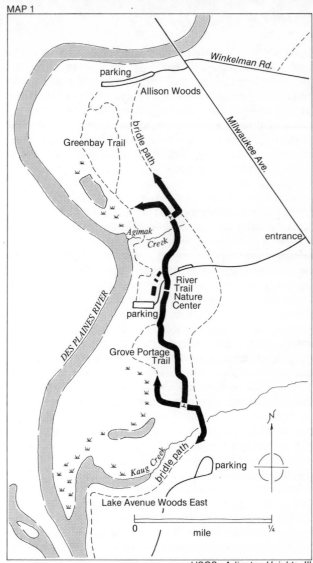

Winkelman Rd.

parking

Allison Woods

Milwaukee Ave.

Greenbay Trail

bridle path

Agimak Creek

entrance

River Trail Nature Center

parking

Grove Portage Trail

DES PLAINES RIVER

N

Kaug Creek

bridle path

parking

Lake Avenue Woods East

0   mile   ¼

USGS: *Arlington Heights, Ill.*

which south of Waterfall Glen has carved a valley more than a mile wide and a hundred feet lower than the adjacent upland. Along the Des Plaines the sluggish river is in places bordered by marshy flats and abandoned channels; the Illinois River, in turn, shows the same erosive features on a far larger scale. Considered together, these varied landscapes exemplify some of the stages by which running water cuts into an elevated region — even if only slightly elevated — and over the ages reduces it to a lower plain.

Stream erosion is the dominant force that shapes the world's landforms. Whenever any part of the earth's crust is raised above sea level, either by uplift of the land or withdrawal of the ocean as water is amassed in continental glaciers, the newly elevated surface is at once subject to the erosive power of running water. Any downward-pitched trough, crevice, or fissure, even though at first shallow or insignificant, is self-aggrandizing, collecting rainwater that falls on other areas. Initially, such minor watercourses are dry between rains, but gradually they deepen with erosion, and once they penetrate the water table, they are fed by a steady seepage of groundwater from the sides of the gullies and ravines.

As a stream extends itself by developing tributaries, its erosive power rapidly increases. The larger drainage area concentrates more water in the channel downstream, where stream energy is swelled both by the greater mass of moving water and by its greater depth, which results in proportionately less friction with the stream bed. In consequence, the speed of the river increases and so does its ability to carry fine clay, silt, and sand in suspension and to push and roll pebbles and cobbles downstream.

Although at first erosion is fastest in the lower reaches of a river where volume is greater, ponds, lakes, and ultimately the ocean constitute a base level below which the stream cannot cut to any significant degree. As downward cutting approaches the base level, the site of the most rapid erosion slowly moves upstream.

MAP 2

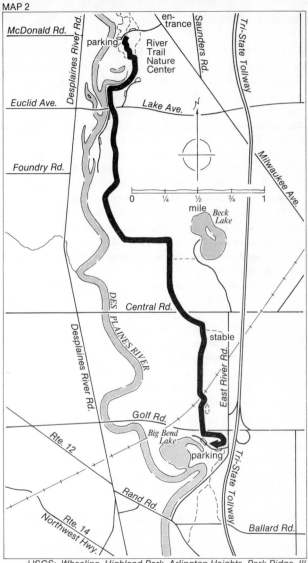

McDonald Rd.

parking

entrance

Saunders Rd.

Tri-State Tollway

Desplaines River Rd.

River Trail Nature Center

Euclid Ave.

Lake Ave.

N

Foundry Rd.

Milwaukee Ave.

0   ¼   ½   ¾   1

mile

Beck Lake

DES PLAINES RIVER

Central Rd.

stable

Desplaines River Rd.

East River Rd.

Golf Rd.

Big Bend Lake

parking

Rte. 12

Tri-State Tollway

Rand Rd.

Rte. 14

Northwest Hwy.

Ballard Rd.

USGS: *Wheeling, Highland Park, Arlington Heights, Park Ridge, Ill.*

Meanwhile, the lower river still possesses great energy. The current erodes the bank wherever the stream is deflected by each slight turn. This tendency to carve wider and wider curves is present along the entire stream but is accentuated in the lower reaches, where downward cutting is no longer possible but where sideward cutting can continue as long as there is flow. Gradually, a meandering course develops as the river snakes back and forth, eroding first one side of the valley and then the other. When sinuosity becomes so extreme that the river doubles back on itself, the current will intercept the channel farther downstream, cutting off the looping meander, as appears to have happened at places along the Des Plaines River (see Maps 2 and 3). Thus, as millenia pass, the river migrates in an ever-changing course over the bottomland, creating a valley much wider than it is deep and leaving behind abandoned channels here and there.

Another distinctive geologic feature develops at the mouth of the river where it empties into an ocean, estuary, or lake. As the current dissipates in the standing water, the capacity of the stream to carry material in suspension is reduced and then eliminated, so that the river's load of gravel, sand, and silt is dropped and forms a delta, as has occurred where the Fox River empties into Grass Lake in northwestern Lake County. Because the current slows gradually, the deposits tend to be sorted, with larger, heavier particles dropped first. After the delta has extended itself a considerable distance in one direction, a flood may cut a new and shorter channel to open water, causing the former course to be abandoned, at least for a period. Deltas typically have several channels or sets of channels among which the stream shifts as deposits are concentrated first in one and then in another.

Examining the variables of stream gradient, valley depth, valley width, and number meanders will indicate the stage of development that has been reached by any stretch of river. In the earliest stage, gullies and ravines eat into the elevated land surface, as exemplified by the numerous ravines along the high

MAP 3

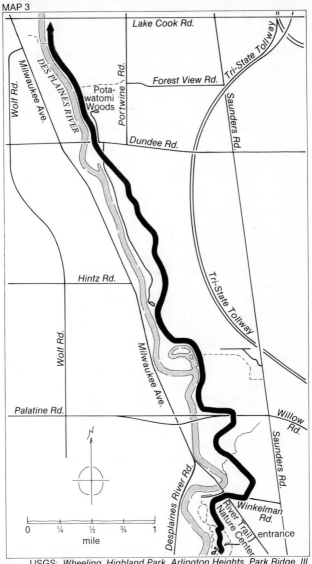

Lake Cook Rd.

Tri-State Tollway

DES PLAINES RIVER

Wolf Rd.

Milwaukee Ave.

Portwine Rd.

Forest View Rd.

Saunders Rd.

Pota-
watomi
Woods

Dundee Rd.

Hintz Rd.

Wolf Rd.

Milwaukee Ave.

Tri-State Tollway

Palatine Rd.

Willow Rd.

Saunders Rd.

N

Desplaines River Rd.

Milwaukee Ave.

Winkelman Rd.

River Trail Nature Center

entrance

0   ¼   ½   ¾   1
mile

USGS: *Wheeling, Highland Park, Arlington Heights, Park Ridge, Ill.*

lakefront in Winnetka, Glencoe, and Highland Park. Because the dominant direction of cutting is downward, the gullies and ravines are steep-sided and V-shaped, eventually becoming major valleys. The gradient of the steambed is steep compared to navigable waterways. Rapids are common. There are no flats in the valley bottom. Valley depth relative to width is at its maximum. Such a stream is said to be in *youth*.

As the stream approaches base level, its gradient diminishes and downward cutting slows. Bends in the course of the stream become accentuated, and the width of the valley increases relative to its depth. At the point where sideward cutting becomes significant and a flat valley floor starts to develop, the stream is said to be in *maturity*.

Finally, when downward cutting has ceased and the stream is at base level, sideward cutting produces a nearly flat and featureless valley, much wider than it is deep, across which the river meanders from side to side. Such an eroded surface is called a *peneplain*. The gradient is low and the broad bottomland is marked only by the scars, swamps, and lakes left by former channels. Perhaps a few rock hummocks and hills — more resistent to erosion than were their surroundings — are left rising above the plain. This stage of river development is *old age*. Meanwhile, the countless gullies and ravines at the river's headwaters remain youthful as they continue to fan outward like the roots of a growing tree, so that the watershed becomes larger and larger, perhaps even intercepting and diverting to itself streams that previously took a different course to the sea.

The terms *youth, maturity,* and *old age* also can be applied to an entire landscape or region to describe the extent to which it has been acted upon by stream erosion. As an upland region experiences the headward erosion of a stream system, more and more of the landscape is given over to a branching network of steep-sided gullies, ravines, and valleys, which gradually widen and develop flat valley bottoms. An area is said to be in youth until about half of the original upland is consumed by valley slopes and the streams are just beginning to develop flats at the valley bottoms. As the percentage of upland diminishes further and the portion in the valley flats increases, the area is in maturity. At some point the upland lying between different tributaries or different stream systems is cut away until the divide changes from a wide, flat summit to a sharp-crested ridge that in turn is worn down to a low, rounded rise. Old age is said to start when more than half of the region is in valley bottom, and it continues as the whole region gradually is reduced to a peneplain. Thus, a general, youth is the time of dominant upland, maturity the time of dominant valley slope, and old age the time of dominant valley bottom.

Such, at any rate, is the general model. Of course, the terms *youth, maturity,* and *old age* do not describe the actual age of a stream or landscape, but only its stage of development. Also, the appearance of any particular stretch of river is determined largely by the durability and structure of the materials through which the stream flows, and the terrain along even a single river can reflect different stages of erosion in no particular sequence, depending on the underlying materials. For example, consider the muted profile of the Des Plaines River as it flows through a region of unconsolidated glacial debris in the vicinity of Chicago, then contrast its low clay banks with the dramatic sandstone cliffs and canyons farther downstream along the Illinois River at Starved Rock. Nonetheless, river systems and local landscapes can be better understood and enjoyed by keeping in mind the general sequence of stream erosion.

Finally, it should be noted that, broadly speaking, the land surface near Chicago is very youthful, since it overwhelmingly consists of glacial deposits that have not yet been stripped away or even greatly altered by stream erosion. So far, most erosion has been concentrated in the immediate vicinity of the region's larger rivers. Compared with much older glaciated areas, where few glacial features remain and the topography is mainly the product of stream erosion, the Chicago region is uneroded and most of the work of the streams lies ahead of them.

AUTOMOBILE: The River Trail follows the Des Plaines River north of Chicago, between Lake Cook Road and Rand Road. The entrance to the River Trail Nature Center is on Milwaukee Avenue 1 mile south of Palatine Road (the westward extension of Willow Road) and 0.8 mile north of Lake Avenue (which becomes Euclid Avenue west of the Des Plaines River). Another nearby major road is Des Plaines River Road, which joins Milwaukee Avenue 0.7 mile north of the entrance to the nature center.

From downtown Chicago take Interstate 90 (Kennedy Expressway) northwest, then switch to Interstate 94 (Edens Expressway) toward Milwaukee. Leave Edens Expressway at the exit for Lake Avenue west. Follow Lake Avenue west 6.2 miles, then turn right onto Milwaukee Avenue. Follow Milwaukee Avenue north 0.8 mile, then turn left into the River Trail Nature Center. Follow the entrance drive 0.3 mile to the parking lots next to the nature center buildings.

From the suburbs north of Chicago, take Edens Expressway south to the exit for Route 41 (Skokie Road) in Wilmette. Turn right (west) onto Lake Avenue and go 6.3 miles, then turn right onto Milwaukee Avenue. Go 0.8 mile, then turn left into the nature center.

If you are approaching from the south on the Tri-State Tollway, the westbound exit at Willow Road also provides easy access to the River Trail Nature Center. Follow Willow Road west 0.5 mile to Saunders Road. Turn left and follow Saunders Road south 0.6 mile, then turn right onto Winkelman Road. Go 0.4 mile to a T-intersection with Milwaukee Avenue. Turn left onto Milwaukee Avenue and go 0.4 mile, then turn right into the nature center.

WALK: There are three short loops, each 0.5 mile long, in the immediate vicinity of the nature center (see Map 1 for this chapter). In addition, it is possible to follow a bridle path south 4 miles along the river to Big Bend Lake (see Map 2) or north 5 miles to Lake Cook Road (see Map 3). Of course, you must also walk back, unless you can arrange a car shuttle. Obviously, a shuttle involves either two cars and two driver-hikers, or a driver who simply meets you at the other end. You can use the maps to shuttle a car to your destination.

For the short Grove Portage Trail circuit or for the bridle path south toward Big Bend Lake, cross the road in front of the nature center building. Turn right in front of the animal pens and follow an asphalt path past some gardens and into the woods. Pass through a gate in a chainlink fence. At a fork in the trail, bear left. At a T-intersection, turn right to return to the nature center parking lot on the Grove Portage Trail, or turn left to head south along the bridle path toward Big Bend Lake. (Incidentally, the signs at this intersection can be misleading, since vandals sometimes tinker with them.)

If you turned left for the bridle path, go 40 yards, then turn right. Pass a picnic area and continue through the woods; soon the Des Plaines River comes into view on the right. With caution, cross Lake/Euclid Avenue and continue on the bridle path through woods and clearings. Eventually, cross Central Road. Pass under high electric transmission lines and cross a railroad. Bear right immediately and continue through the woods. After crossing Golf Road, continue as the trail at first runs parallel with the road toward the left, then curves right to cross the entrance to the Big Bend Lake parking lot, which is a good place to leave a car if you can arrange a car shuttle. As shown on the map, it is possible to continue farther south, but various local roads, the tollway, and noise from O'Hare Airport impinge on the trail.

As noted earlier, the bridle path also leads north from the vicinity of the nature center. Cross the road in front of the nature center building, then turn left in front of the animal pens. Cross the entrance road. Pass through a gate in a chainlink fence and continue through the woods to a trail intersection 20 yards beyond a short footbridge. At this intersection, you can either continue straight to return to the nature center parking lot via a short trail circuit, or you can turn right to join the bridle path that leads north along the river.

If you turned right for the bridle path, go 30 yards, then turn left. Follow the bridle path through the woods and past a field. Continue to a parking lot for Allison Woods. Turn right and follow the entrance drive to Milwaukee Avenue, visible 170 yards away. With caution, cross Milwaukee Avenue, then continue straight away from Milwaukee Avenue on the shoulder of Winkelman Road.

Follow Winkelman Road 280 yards, then turn left into the woods on a bridle path. Cross a bridge over Willow Road and continue as the main path bears left, then later turns right. Soon the Des Plaines River comes into view on the left. Continue straight past a trail intersecting from the right. Pass a parking lot and a picnic area on the left. Continue through the woods for more than a mile. Eventually, cross a park road. Continue through the woods to Dundee Road.

With caution, cross Dundee Road and continue through the woods on the bridle path, which soon follows the river's edge. The parking lot for Potawatomi Woods on the right is a good place to leave a car if you can arrange a shuttle. Or, as shown on the map, you can continue north along the river all the way to Lake Cook Road, but there is no parking lot there.

5

WATERFALL GLEN FOREST PRESERVE

Walking or ski touring — 9 miles (14.5 kilometers). The trail circles through rolling terrain, occasionally passing ponds, marshes, and steep ravines. Woods alternate with prairie and overgrown fields. Open daily from dawn until dusk. Managed by the Forest Preserve District of DuPage County. Telephone (312) 790-4900 or 790-1558.

WATERFALL GLEN FOREST PRESERVE surrounds Argonne National Laboratory, which is known for research in atomic physics and related fields. The long walk described here follows a trail loop through woods and meadows that form a buffer zone around the research center, but neither the Argonne buildings nor the surrounding highways and residential developments can be seen from the trail.

DuPage County first began to purchase land at Waterfall Glen in 1925, when it bought a few scenic areas, including the ravine at Sawmill Creek, where the Civilian Conservation Corps constructed a small waterfall during the 1930s. Most of the land, however, was acquired decades later as a gift from the federal government under the Legacy of Parks Program, by which surplus federal land throughout the nation was transferred to local governments for park use. A doughnut-shaped area containing 2,222 acres around the perimeter of Argonne National Laboratory was conveyed to the local forestry district in 1973, making Waterfall Glen, at a total of 2,433 acres, the largest of DuPage County's three dozen forest preserves.

The terrain at Waterfall Glen is more varied than in many areas near Chicago. At the trail head in the northern part of the reservation, the land surface is slightly rolling, formed by a thick but uneven layer of clay, sand, pebbles and cobbles called *glacial till*. This material was left as a blanket covering the landscape when the Wisconsinan glacier retreated from the Chicago region about 12,500 years ago. As the trail circles to the southwest, it passes a large marsh and other shallow depressions (called *kettles*) created when blocks of glacial ice that were imbedded in the till melted away. Steep ravines are encountered at the walk's midpoint where streams descend abruptly to the valley of the Des Plaines River, which borders Waterfall Glen to the south. The result is terrain described as "broken" by the surveyors of the Geodetic Survey in the 1840s — broken by numerous ravines, ridges, and rock outcrops. Finally, as the trail circles east and north, it returns gradually to the upland of glacial till, dotted with isolated ponds and marshes.

The valley of the Des Plaines River in the vicinity of Waterfall Glen is more than a mile wide and a hundred feet lower that the upland immediately adjacent to it. The large valley reflects the erosive power of what once was a far bigger river than that seen today. As the Wisconsinan ice sheet receded, the Des Plaines River was fed by a huge volume of meltwater. For a period even Lake Michigan drained to the southwest through the valley of the Des Plaines. South of present-day Waterfall Glen, the Des Plaines River penetrated to bedrock and scoured the valley floor to create a bedrock plain. Bedrock is also visible in the tributary ravines, as at Sawmill Creek in the vicinity of the waterfall.

The bedrock visible in places at Waterfall Glen is dolomite, a particularly durable variety of limestone. These strata were deposited as sediments between 500 and 400 million years ago when the low interior of the continent was flooded by a shallow sea extending from the Gulf of Mexico to Alaska. Limestone, of course, is a common building material, and at Waterfall

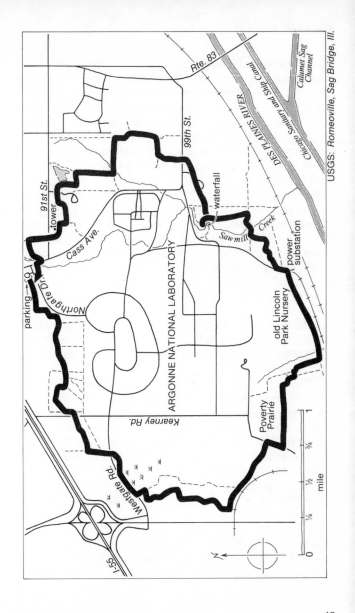

USGS: *Romeoville, Sag Bridge, Ill.*

Glen, quarrying became a major industry during the 1860s. Edwin Walker, a Chicago builder, operated three quarries for limestone — or Athens Marble, as it was called — within what is now the forest preserve. The limestone for the Chicago Water Tower, built by Walker in 1869, was quarried at Waterfall Glen.

Lumbering was another important local industry. From 1860 through the 1880s, the Ward brothers' sawmill occupied a site on Sawmill Creek, although the stream was then called Hennebry's Creek.

And speaking of names brings us finally to Waterfall Glen. The small dell by the man-made waterfall on Sawmill Creek has long been known as Rocky Glen, but in 1973, when more than two thousand additional acres were acquired from the federal government, the entire forest preserve was named not for the waterfall but in honor of Seymour "Bud" Waterfall, president of the forest preserve district's Board of Commissioners from 1953 to 1959.

AUTOMOBILE: Waterfall Glen Forest Preserve surrounds Argonne National Laboratory southwest of Chicago. The entrance is on Cass Avenue 1.5 miles south of Interstate 55.

From Chicago — or from the Tri-State Tollway — take Interstate 55 (Stevenson Expressway) south toward St. Louis. Leave I-55 at the exit for Cass Avenue south toward Argonne National Laboratory. (This exit is 4 miles southwest of the Tri-State Tollway.) Follow Cass Avenue south about 1.5 miles, then turn right onto Northgate Drive. (Northgate Drive is immediately after an octagonal structure at the top of a knoll.) Follow Northgate Drive for only 100 yards, then turn right into the parking lot for Waterfall Glen Forest Preserve.

WALK: Locate the trail where it enters the woods behind an information board and picnic area. Head straight through the woods, crossing another trail immediately.

WATERFALL GLEN

Cross a small bridge and continue on a wide, grassy path marked with green, orange, blue, and red blazes. Follow the wide, grassy path as it zigzags left uphill, right in front of a road, then left and right. Continue straight into the woods where another grassy path intersects from the left. Cross or pass several fire lanes, in each case staying on the red-blazed trail where the green, orange, and blue trails successively turn off to the side. Continue through woods and scrub on a wide, grassy path.

Eventually, follow the path parallel with a road (Kearney Road) on the right, then bear half-right across an abandoned stretch of road. Continue through pine woods, then bear left at a T-intersection. Go straight past a trail intersecting from the left and past a chainlink fence on the left. Cross Westgate Road next to a gate, then turn right on the blazed trail. Continue through scrub, with the road visible now and again on the right. Emerge from the scrub and follow the road shoulder past a marsh on the left.

Immediately past the marsh, turn left into the woods, then turn sharply right at the next trail junction to continue on the red-blazed trail. Bear left at the next intersection. Eventually, at a T-intersection in front of a railroad, turn left.

With the railroad on the right, continue past a trail intersecting from the left. Follow a rutted gravel track across a weedy field. Turn right at a gravel road, then left at the next intersection by an information board. (Note that here and for the rest of the circuit, the trail markers are fiberglass stakes blazed with orange disks.)

Continue past fields and scrubby growth — what a park brochure calls Poverty Prairie. Zigzag right, left, then right to follow the main track through the woods. Bear left, then right to follow the trail markers past intersections, then continue on the wide trail through the woods.

At a T-intersection, turn left downhill. Follow a rutted road, at first with a railroad on the right, then along a hillside and eventually past the retaining walls of the old

Lincoln Park Nursery. At an intersection near a power substation, turn left. Follow a gravel road 130 yards (passing another gravel, rutted road intersecting from the right), then bear right to follow the trail markers uphill and into the woods. Continue as the trail zigzags through the woods. At the broad swath of a gas pipeline right-of-way, turn right. Cross Sawmill Creek on a footbridge, then fork left in 50 yards to follow a flight of steps uphill. About 35 yards past the crest of the hill, turn left. (If you pass a chainlink enclosure for pipeline valves, you have gone too far.) Follow a rutted gravel track, which eventually borders a ravine on the left. At an information board, fork left to follow a spur trail along the top of the bluff, then downhill and to the left to reach Rocky Glen and a small waterfall.

From the waterfall, return to the information board at the top of the bluff and continue around the trail circuit. Cross a gravel road and continue straight into the woods on the other side. At an asphalt road, continue straight on the road shoulder. Just before reaching a house on the right, turn right into the woods.

Follow the trail through the woods and across 99th Street. Turn right at a trail intersection, then left at the next junction to follow the markers along a wide, grassy swath. Within sight of some houses on the right, turn left onto another wide swath through the woods. After crossing a brook, turn right to continue on a broad, grassy fire lane. Watch for a narrow trail intersecting from the left about 75 yards before the wide fire lane bends right; turn left onto the narrow trail and follow it through the woods, then sharply right. Eventually, pass between a swamp on the left and a pond on the right, then turn sharply left.

Cross a park road and continue straight, then left and right along the edge of the woods. Continue straight into a pine plantation. At a T-intersection, turn right, then left to pass a tower. Cross 91st Street and continue on a wide, grassy trail. Pass through mature woods, then an area of scrub and young woods. Watch for a grassy path on the left, just before more mature woods; turn left here and follow the path along the edge of a pine plantation. Bear left where another trail intersects from the right.

At Cass Avenue, turn right across a bridge, then turn left across the road and into the woods on a grassy trail. Cross Northgate Drive and continue through the woods. Turn right at a T-intersection in order to return to the parking lot at the trail head.

6

PALOS HILLS FOREST PRESERVE
northeast section

Walking or ski touring — 5.5 miles (8.9 kilometers). Starting at the Little Red Schoolhouse Nature Center, follow a bridle path through woods dotted with meadows, marshes, and ponds. As shown on the map, several shorter footpaths also start from the nature center. The parking lot and short footpaths at the nature center are open Monday through Thursday 9:00 A.M. to 4:30 P.M. and from 9:00 A.M. to 5:00 P.M. on Saturday, Sunday, and holidays. The nature center is closed Friday, Thanksgiving, Christmas, and New Year's Day. Dogs are prohibited at the nature center. The large network of bridle paths is open daily from dawn until dusk. If you plan to walk on the bridle paths early in the morning or late in the afternoon, park your car in the Country Lane Woods lot off 95th Street between 96th Avenue and 104th Avenue, as shown on the map. Managed by the Forest Preserve District of Cook County. Telephone (312) 261-8400 from the city or 366-9420 from the suburbs.

BECAUSE OF THE VARIETY of its habitats — deciduous woods, thickets, meadows, swamps, marshes, and numerous ponds and lakes — the Palos Hills Forest Preserve is among the better places near Chicago to see a wide assortment of birds. According to the booklet *Chicagoland Birds,* compiled by Ellen Thorne Smith and published by the Field Museum of Natural History, numerous waterfowl congregate on the ponds at Palos Hills as soon as the ice melts, and many remain until

the water freezes over in the fall. Nesting birds include grebes, rails, gallinules, and four species of herons. Of course, to see the greatest number of species, spring and fall migrations are the best seasons of the year and dawn is the best time of day.

Even for fledgling birders, identifying the many species that nest in the Chicago area or pass through during migration is easier than might at first be thought. Shape, size, plumage, and other physical characteristics are distinguishing field marks. Range, season, habitat, song, and behavior are other useful keys to identifying birds.

Range is of primary importance for the simple reason that many birds are not found throughout North America or even the Midwest, but only in certain regions such as the Atlantic and Gulf coasts. For example, cedar waxwings and Bohemian waxwings closely resemble each other, so it helps to know that cedar waxwings are fairly common near Chicago, whereas Bohemian waxwings are rare (although they are common in the Northwest). A good field guide provides range maps based on years of reported sightings and bird counts. Of course, bird ranges are not static: some pioneering species, such as the glossy ibis and house finch, have extended their ranges during recent decades. Other birds, such as the ivory-billed woodpecker, have lost ground and may even have died out.

Season is related to range, since migratory birds appear in different parts of their ranges during different times of year. The five species of spotted-breasted thrushes, for instance, are sometimes difficult to distinguish from each other; all are common in the Chicago area during spring and fall migrations, yet all but the wood thrush are rare during summer. Again, the maps in most field guides reflect this sort of information, and a detailed account of seasonal occurrence is set forth in *Chicagoland Birds*.

Habitat is important in identifying birds. Even before you spot a bird, the surroundings can tell you what species you are likely to see. Within its range a species usually appears only in certain preferred habitats, although during migration some

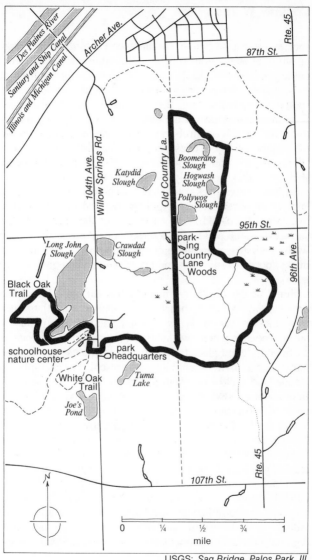

Des Plaines River
Sanitary and Ship Canal
Illinois and Michigan Canal
Archer Ave.

Rte. 45

87th St.

104th Ave.
Willow Springs Rd.

Old Country La.

Katydid Slough

Boomerang Slough
Hogwash Slough
Pollywog Slough

95th St.

96th Ave.

Long John Slough
Crawdad Slough

park-ing
Country Lane Woods

Black Oak Trail

schoolhouse-nature center

White Oak Trail

Joe's Pond

park headquarters

Tuma Lake

Rte. 45

107th St.

N

0   ¼   ½   ¾   1
mile

USGS: Sag Bridge, Palos Park, Ill.

57

species are less particular. (In many cases, birds show a degree of physical adaptation to their preferred environment.) As its name implies, the marsh wren is seldom found far from cattails, rushes, sedges, or tall marsh grasses; if a wrenlike bird is spotted in such a setting, it is unlikely to be a house wren or Carolina wren or one of the other species commonly found in thick underbrush or shrubbery. Ducks can be difficult to identify unless you tote a telescope; but even if all you can see is a silhouette, you can start with the knowledge that shallow marshes and creeks normally attract few diving ducks (such as oldsquaw, canvasbacks, redheads, ring-necked ducks, greater and lesser scaup, common goldeneye, and buffleheads) and that large, deep bodies of water are not the usual setting for surface-feeding puddle ducks (American black ducks, gadwalls, mallards, common pintails, American widgeons, wood ducks, northern shovelers, and blue-winged and green-winged teals).

Some of the distinctive habitats that different bird species prefer are open ocean; beaches; salt marsh; mud flats; meadows; thickets; various types of woods; and creeks, ponds, and lakes. The area where two habitats join, called an *ecotone,* is a particularly good place to look for birds because species peculiar to either environment might be present. For example, both meadowlarks and wood warblers might be found where a hay field abuts a forest. All good field guides provide information on habitat preferences that can help to locate a species or to assess the likelihood of a tentative identification.

Song announces the identity (or at least the location) of birds even before they are seen. Although some species, such as the red-winged blackbird, have only a few songs, others, such as the mockingbird, have an infinite variety. Some birds, most notably thrushes, sing different songs in the morning and evening. In many species the basic songs vary among individuals and also from one area to another, giving rise to regional "dialects." Nonetheless, the vocal repertory of most songbirds is sufficiently constant in timbre and pattern to identify each species simply by its songs.

Bird songs, as distinguished from calls, can be very complex. They are sung only by the male of most species, usually in spring and summer. The male arrives first at the breeding and nesting area after migration. He stakes out a territory for courting, mating, and nesting by singing at prominent points around the area's perimeter, which wards off intrusion by other males of his species and simultaneously attracts females. On the basis of the male's display or the desirability of his territory, the female selects her mate. Experiments suggests that female birds build nests faster and lay more eggs when exposed to the songs of males with a larger vocal repertory than others of their species, and the relative volume of their songs appears to be a way for males to establish status among themselves.

In a few species, including eastern bluebirds, "Baltimore" orioles, cardinals, and white-throated sparrows, both sexes sing, although the males are more active in defending their breeding territory. Among mockingbirds, both sexes sing in fall and winter, but only males sing in spring and summer. Some birds, such as canaries, have different songs for different seasons.

Birds tend to heed the songs of their own kind and to ignore the songs of other species, which do not compete for females nor, in many cases, for the same type of nesting materials or food. In consequence, a single area might include the overlapping breeding territories of several species. From year to year such territories are bigger or smaller, depending on the food supply. Typically, most small songbirds require about half an acre from which others of their species are excluded.

Bird calls (as distinguished from songs) are short, simple, sometimes harsh, and used by both males and females at all times of year to communicate alarm, aggression, location, and existence of food. Nearly all birds have some form of call. Warning calls often are heeded by species other than the caller's. Some warning calls are thin, high-pitched whistles that are difficult to locate and so do not reveal the bird's location to predators. Birds also use mobbing calls to summon other birds, as chickadees and crows do when scolding and harassing owls and other unwanted visitors. Birds flying in flocks, like cedar waxwings, often call continuously. Such calls help birds that migrate by night to stay together.

The study of bird dialects and experiments with birds that have been deafened or raised in isolation indicate that songs are genetically inherited only to a very crude extent. Although a few species, such as doves, sing well even when raised in isolation, most birds raised alone produce inferior, simplified songs. Generally, young songbirds learn their songs by listening to adult birds and by practice singing, called *subsong*. Birds raised in isolation and exposed to many tape-recorded songs show an innate preference for the songs of their own species.

Probably the easiest way to learn bird songs is to listen repeatedly to recordings and to refer at the same time to a standard field guide. Most guides describe bird vocalizations with such terms as *harsh, nasal, flutelike, piercing, plaintive, wavering, twittering, buzzing, sneezy,* and *sputtering*. Played slowly, bird recordings demonstrate that the songs contain many more notes than the human ear ordinarily hears.

Shape is one of the first and most important aspects to notice once you actually see a bird. Most birds can at least be placed in the proper family and many species can be identified by shape or silhouette, without reference to other field marks. Some birds, such as kestrels, are distinctly stocky, big-headed, and powerful-looking, while others, such as catbirds and cuckoos, are elegantly long and slender. Kingfishers, blue jays, tufted titmice, Bohemian and cedar waxwings, and cardinals are among the few birds with crests.

Bird bills frequently have distinctive shapes and more than any other body part show adaptation to food supply. The beak can be chunky like that of a grosbeak, which cracks seeds; thin and curved like that of a creeper, which probes bark for insects; hooked like that of a shrike, which tears at flesh; long and slender like that of a hummingbird, which sips nectar from tubular flowers; or some other characteristic shape depending on the bird's food. Goatsuckers, swifts, flycatchers, and swallows, all of which catch flying insects, have widely hinged bills and gaping mouths. The long, thin bills of starlings and meadowlarks are suited to probing the ground. In the Galapagos Islands west of Ecuador, Charles Darwin noted fourteen species of finches, each of which had evolved a different type of beak or style of feeding that gave it a competitive advantage for a particular type of food. Many birds are nonetheless flexible about their diet, especially from season to season when food sources change or become scarce. For example, Tennessee warblers, which ordinarily glean insects from foliage, also take large amounts of nectar from tropical flowers when wintering in South and Central America.

In addition to beaks, nearly every other part of a bird's body is adapted to help exploit its environment. Feet of passerines, or songbirds, are adapted to perching, with three toes in front and one long toe behind; waterfowl have webbed or lobed feet for swimming; and raptors have talons for grasping prey.

Other key elements of body shape are the length and form of wings, tails, and legs. The wings may be long, pointed, and developed for swift, sustained flight, like those of falcons. Or the wings may be short and rounded for abrupt bursts of speed, like those of accipiters. The tail may have a deep fork like that of a barn swallow, a shallow notch like that of a tree swallow, a square tip like that of a cliff swallow, or a round tip like that of a blue jay.

Size is difficult to estimate and therefore not very useful in identifying birds. The best approach is to bear in mind the relative sizes of different species and to use certain well-known birds like the chickadee, sparrow, robin, kingfisher, and crow

as standards for mental comparison. For example, if a bird resembles a song sparrow but looks unusually large, it might be a fox sparrow.

Plumage, whether plain or princely, muted or magnificent, is one of the most obvious keys to identification. Color can occur in remarkable combinations of spots, stripes, streaks, patches, and other patterns that make even supposedly drab birds a pleasure to see. In some instances, like the brown streaks of American bitterns and many other species, the plumage provides camouflage. Most vireos and warblers are various shades and combinations of yellow, green, brown, gray, and black, as one would expect from their forest environment. The black and white backs of woodpeckers help them to blend in with bark dappled with sunlight. The bold patterns of kill-deers and some other plovers break up their outlines in much the same manner that warships used to be camouflaged. Many shore birds display countershading: they are dark above and light below, a pattern that reduces the effect of shadows and makes them appear an inconspicuous monotone. Even some brightly colored birds have camouflaging plumages when they are young and least able to avoid predators.

For some species, it is important *not* to be camouflaged. Many sea birds are mostly white, which in all light conditions enables them to be seen at great distances against the water. Because flocks of sea birds spread out from their colonies to search for food, it is vital that a bird that has located food be visible to others after it has landed on the water to feed.

To organize the immense variation of plumages, focus on different basic elements and ask the following types of questions. Starting with the head, is it uniformly colored like that of the red-headed woodpecker? Is there a small patch on the crown, like that of Wilson's warbler and the ruby-crowned kinglet, or a larger cap on the front and top of the head, like that of the common redpoll and American goldfinch? Is the crown striped like the ovenbird's? Does a ring surround the eye, as with a Connecticut warbler, or are the eye rings perhaps even joined across the top of the bill to form spectacles, like those of a yellow-breasted chat? Is there a stripe over or through the eyes, like the red-breasted nuthatch's, or a conspicuous black mask across the eyes, like that of a common yellowthroat or loggerhead shrike? From the head go on to the rest of the body, where distinctive colors and patterns can also mark a bird's bill, throat, breast, belly, back, sides, wings, rump, tail, and legs.

Finally, what a bird *does* is an important clue to its identity. Certain habits, postures, ways of searching for food, and other behavior characterize different species. Some passerines, such as larks, juncos, and towhees, are strictly ground feeders; other birds, including flycatchers and swallows, nab insects on the wing; and others, such as nuthatches and creepers, glean insects from the crevices in bark. Woodpeckers bore into the bark. Vireos and most warblers pick insects from the foliage of trees and brush.

All these birds may be further distinguished by other habits of eating. For example, towhees scratch for insects and seeds by kicking backward with both feet together, whereas juncos rarely do, although both hop to move along the ground. Other ground feeders, such as meadowlarks, walk rather than hop. Despite the children's song, robins generally run, not hop. Swallows catch insects while swooping and skimming in continuous flight, but flycatchers dart out from a limb, grab an insect (sometimes with an audible smack), and then return to their perch. Brown creepers have the curious habit of systematically searching for food by climbing trees in spirals, then flying back to the ground to climb again. Woodpeckers tend to hop upward, bracing themselves against the tree with their stiff tails. Nuthatches walk up and down trees and braches head first, seemingly without regard for gravity. Vireos are sluggish compared to the hyperactive, flitting warblers.

Many birds divide a food source into zones, an arrangement that apparently evolved to ensure each species its own food supply. The short-legged green heron sits at the edge of the water or on a low overhanging branch, waiting for its prey to come close to shore. The medium-sized black-crowned and yellow-crowned night herons hunt in shallow water. The long-legged great blue heron stalks fish in water up to two feet deep. Swans, geese, and many ducks graze underwater on the stems and tubers of grassy plants, but the longer necks of swans and geese enable them to reach deeper plants. Similarly, different species of shore birds take food from the same mud flat by probing with their varied bills to different depths. Species of warblers that feed in the same tree are reported to concentrate in separate areas among the trunk, twig tips, tree top, and ground. Starlings and cowbirds feeding in flocks on the ground show another arrangement that provides an even distribution of food: those in the rear fly ahead to the front, so that the entire flock rolls slowly across the field.

Different species also have different styles of flight. Soaring is typical of some big birds. Gulls float nearly motionless in the wind. Buteos and turkey vultures soar on updrafts in wide circles, although turkey vultures may be further distinguished by wings held in a shallow V. Some other large birds, such as accipiters, rarely soar but instead interrupt their wing beats with glides. Kestrels, terns, and kingfishers can hover in one spot. Hummingbirds, like oversized dragonflies, also can hover and even fly backward. Slightly more erratic than the swooping, effortless flight of swallows is that of swifts, flitting with wing beats that appear to alternate (but do not). Still other birds, such as the American goldfinch and flickers, dip up and down in wavelike flight. Some species, including jays and grackles, fly dead straight. Among ducks, the surface-feeding species launch themselves directly upward into flight, seeming to jump from the water, but the heavy diving ducks typically patter along the surface before becoming airborne.

Various idiosyncracies distinguish yet other species. The spotted sandpiper and northern waterthrush walk with a teetering, bobbing motion. Coots pump their heads back and forth as they swim. The eastern phoebe regularly jerks its tail downward while perching, but wrens often cock their tails vertically. Herons and egrets fly with their necks folded back; storks, ibises, and cranes fly with their necks outstretched. Still other birds have characteristic postures while sitting or flying or other unique habits that provide a reliable basis for identification.

AUTOMOBILE: The Palos Hills are located southwest of Chicago across the Des Plaines River from Argonne National Laboratory. The entrance to the Little Red Schoolhouse Nature Center, where this walk begins, is on 104th Avenue, 0.5 mile south of the junction with 95th Street.

From Chicago take Interstate 55 (Stevenson Expressway) south toward St. Louis. Leave I-55 at the exit for Routes 12, 20, and 45 south (LaGrange Road). Follow Routes 12, 20, and 45 south 3.4 miles, then turn right onto 95th Street. Go 1.3 miles, then turn left onto 104th Avenue (Willow Springs Road). Go 0.5 mile to the entrance to the Little Red Schoolhouse Nature Center on the right.

From the suburbs north, west, and south of Chicago, the Tri-State Tollway provides good access to the Palos Hills. Leave the tollway for Interstate 55 (Stevenson Expressway) north toward Chicago. At the next exit, leave I-55 for Routes 12, 20, and 45 south (LaGrange Road). Follow Routes 12, 20, and 45 south for 3.2 miles, then turn right onto 95th Street. Go 1.3 miles, then turn left onto 104th Avenue (Willow Springs Road). Go 0.5 mile to the entrance to the Little Red Schoolhouse Nature Center on the right.

WALK: For a loop of only 1.8 miles on the Black Oak Trail (part of which borders Long John Slough), go to the right of the schoolhouse on a path leading to the water's edge. Continue with Long John Slough on the right. At the next two trail junctions, fork right for the Black Oak Trail circuit, which eventually returns to the schoolhouse.

For a longer walk of 5.5 miles through woods and past ponds and swamps east of 104th Avenue, join a path almost directly opposite the front of the schoolhouse. Go 140 yards to a four-way trail junction with a bridle path. Turn left and follow the bridle path across 104th Avenue. Continue as the trail curves left parallel with the road, then right past the park headquarters compound.

Follow the broad bridle path as it curves through the woods. (Ignore all narrow footpaths intersecting from left and right.) Continue straight through an oblique four-way intersection. (You will return later by the bridle path intersecting from the left.)

Follow the broad bridle path as it curves through the woods, at one point passing a trail intersecting from the right. Eventually, cross 95th Street. Continue through the woods and past Hogwash Slough on the left. At a four-way trail junction, turn left. Pass Boomerang Slough on the left, then turn left at a T-intersection onto a straight bridle path (old Country Lane). Follow Country Lane south back across 95th Street and across a road connecting two parking lots at Country Lane Woods. Eventually, at a four-way trail junction, turn sharply right to return to the nature center by the path that you took earlier in the opposite direction.

7

PALOS HILLS FOREST PRESERVE
southern section

Walking or ski touring — 4 miles (6.4 kilometers). The trail explores the bluff and wooded highlands that overlook the Sag Channel, through which Lake Michigan once drained to the southwest. A longer excursion is possible by following trails to the east of 96th Avenue, as shown on the map. Open daily from dawn until dusk. Managed by the Forest Preserve District of Cook County. Telephone (312) 261-8400 from the city or 366-9420 from the suburbs.

WHEN I WAS A CHILD growing up near Chicago, I sometimes took a shovel — a real one, not a toy — to the beach, where I liked to play in a small stream that flowed across the sand and into the lake. First I would dam the stream; the dam, however, had to be very long because the beach was flat and the impounded water quickly spread to form a large pool. Eventually, of course, the water overflowed at one point or another, and a trickle rapidly became a torrent that washed a big hole in my dam. When all was done, what was left was a rivulet flowing across the sand as before, except that at one point the stream passed through a wide gap in the long, low, irregular ridge that had been my dam.

Something like this happened on a larger scale — a *much* larger scale — at the Palos Hills about 12,500 years ago, only then the dam was a long glacial moraine of which the Palos Hills are part, and the impounded water was glacial Lake Chicago, the predecessor of Lake Michigan. At the Palos Hills,

the lake overflowed and broke through the moraine, carving an immense gap through the hills in the area explored by this walk.

Since the onset of the Ice Age — or Pleistocene Epoch — in North America about one million years ago, the Chicago area has been subjected to four major glaciations. In each case the ice sheets originated in the Hudson Bay region of northern Canada and from there spread in all directions. During each incursion of the continental glaciers, the erosive action of immense lobes of ice widened and deepened the basins now occupied by the Great Lakes, which previously may have been broad lowlands created by an extensive river system. At their farthest advance, the glaciers extended beyond the margins of the present lakes, covering most of Illinois and Indiana, for example. Between episodes of glaciation, which lasted perhaps 50,000 to 70,000 years, were longer periods of 200,000 or 300,000 years, during which the climate became warmer and the glaciers retreated northward.

The most recent glacier to invade Illinois is termed the Wisconsinan glacier; it advanced about 70,000 years ago and retreated from the Chicago region about 12,500 years ago. As the glacier melted, an immense quantity of clay, sand, pebbles, and boulders that had been picked up and carried within the ice was dumped in an uneven blanket over the landscape. During its retreat, the glacier also left behind long ridges called *end moraines*. These formed where the rate at which the ice front melted was matched by the glacier's forward movement, so that for a period the ice margin was more or less stationary. In consequence, debris from the melting glacier accumulated in a range of hills along the entire ice front, like piles of sand and gravel at the end of a conveyor belt. The landscape of Illinois shows dozens of ridges running more or less parallel with each other and with the shore of Lake Michigan; on a map they appear to be arranged in festoons drooping far into southern Illinois and Indiana.

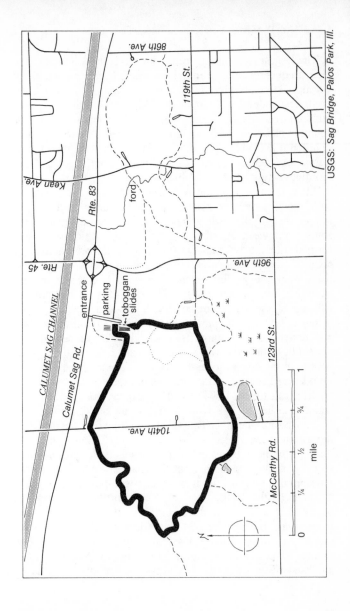

USGS: Sag Bridge, Palos Park, Ill.

86th Ave.

119th St.

Kean Ave.

Rte. 83

ford

Rte. 45

96th Ave.

CALUMET SAG CHANNEL

entrance

parking

toboggan slides

Calumet Sag Rd.

123rd St.

104th Ave.

McCarthy Rd.

N

0   ¼   ½   ¾   1
mile

71

The largest end moraine near Chicago is the Valpariso Moraine, frequently called a morainic system because it actually is composed of nine ridges lying in close proximity. At its highest point near Valpariso, Indiana, the Valpariso Moraine rises two hundred feet above Lake Michigan. It extends around the southern end of the lake in a large, U-shaped band of hills more than ten miles wide. The Palos Hills, which show the random hummocks, hollows, marshes, and ponds characteristic of end moraines, are part of the Valpariso Moraine.

After formation of the Valpariso Moraine, the meltwater from the Wisconsinan glacier was trapped between the receding ice sheet to the north and the dike-like moraine to the east, south, and west. A lake — glacial Lake Chicago — was formed, rising to a height sixty feet above the present average level of Lake Michigan. A terrace and ridge of sand delineate the former beach. Termed the Glenwood beach, this ancient shoreline still is discernible today in many places. In the Chicago region, the Glenwood beach is located inland as much as ten miles from the present beach; the site of all of Chicago was under water, although Blue Island, lying immediately to the south of the city, was indeed an island. Silt settled to the bottom of the lake to form the thick bed of lacustrine clay now found near the land surface throughout most of the city.

Brim full to overflowing with meltwater from the Wisconsinan ice sheet, Lake Chicago found an outlet through the Valpariso Moraine at the Palos Hills. Spilling over the moraine, the torrent carved a gap — now called the Chicago Outlet — through the heights. Actually, two channels developed in the vicinity of the Palos Hills, but the channels merged half way through the moraine to form a configuration resembling a Y tilted to the right, thus: ∠. The northern arm now is occupied by a section of the Des Plaines River; the eastern arm is occupied by the Calumet Sag Channel. The two valleys merge just west of the Palos Hills and from there the Des Plaines River continues southwest through the Valpariso Moraine past Waterfall Glen (see Chapter 5). With the Des Plaines

River to the north, the Sag Channel to the south, and glacial Lake Chicago to the east, the portion of the Palos Hills embraced by the arms of the Y was an island, now called Mt. Forest Island (although, of course, it is no longer an island). On a larger scale, water from the Lake Huron basin flowed through the Grand River Valley across central Michigan and into Lake Chicago, swelling the torrent that ultimately drained through the Chicago Outlet.

As the channel through the Valpariso Moraine got deeper, the level of Lake Chicago fell. For reasons that are the subject of ongoing debate among geologists, the drop in water level did not continue at a steady rate. Instead, after falling twenty feet, the level stabilized and another beach — the Calumet beach — was formed. For a period Lake Chicago stood at the Calumet level, but about 11,000 years ago, rapid erosion in the Chicago Outlet resulted in another twenty-foot drop in lake level. Yet another beach — the Toleston beach — was formed at the new level.

Lake Chicago remained at the Toleston level and continued to drain through the Palos Hills until a lower outlet to the north through the Straits of Mackinac was uncovered by withdrawal of the ice sheet about 9,500 years ago, at which time the lake fell seventy feet, far below its current level. This low level was possible because the land surface east of Lake Huron (in the vicinity of present-day Lake Nipissing and the Ottawa River) had been greatly depressed by the weight of the ice, thus providing an outlet to the St. Lawrence Valley that bypassed Lake Erie, Niagara Falls, and Lake Ontario. However, relieved of its burden of ice, the land gradually rebounded. The outlet through the Ottawa River was closed, and Lake Michigan and Lake Huron returned to the Toleston level. In consequence, water again discharged through the Chicago Outlet between 4,000 and 3,000 years ago. At the same time, a new gap (termed the St. Clair Outlet) was eroded past the site of present-day Detroit at the southern end of Lake Huron. Because the St. Clair Outlet was through unconsolidated clay, sand, and cobbles, erosion there progressed more rapidly than at the Chicago Outlet, which had long before reached the stratum of bedrock seen today at the bottom of the Des Plaines Valley downstream from the Palos Hills. As erosion continued in the St. Clair Outlet, the Chicago Outlet was abandoned, and Lake Michigan and Lake Huron gradually fell another twenty feet to their present level, which was reached about 2,000 years ago.

Of course, the gap through the Valpariso Moraine still carries the Des Plaines River, but the stream is a mere shadow of the torrent that carved the valley through the hills. And except for the Calumet Sag Channel and a few sloughs, the Sag Valley is now dry, although the steep bluff and wide bottomland clearly indicate that a major river once coursed through the valley. Now part of Cook County's largest forest preserve, the bluff and bordering heights are traversed by the walk described below. Also, given snow, the bluff provides an excellent opportunity for tobogganing on the chutes at Swallow Cliff.

AUTOMOBILE: The Palos Hills are located southwest of Chicago across the Des Plaines River from Argonne National Laboratory. The entrance to the Swallow Cliff parking lot, where this walk begins, is on Route 83 only 0.2 mile west of the intersection with Route 45 (96th Avenue).

From Chicago take Interstate 55 (Stevenson Expressway) south toward St. Louis. Leave I-55 at the exit for Routes 12, 20, and 45 south (LaGrange Road). Focusing on Route 45 in particular (Routes 12 and 20 turn east at 95th Street), follow Route 45 south 5.7 miles. Immediately after crossing a short bridge over the Calumet Sag Channel, turn right onto Route 83 northbound. Follow Route 83 (Calumet Sag Road) 0.2 mile, then turn left into the Swallow Cliff Toboggan Slide and Winter Sports Area.

From the suburbs north, west, and south of Chicago, the Tri-State Tollway provides good access to the Palos

Hills. Leave the tollway for Interstate 55 (Stevenson Expressway) north toward Chicago. At the next exit, leave I-55 for Routes 12, 20, and 45 south (LaGrange Road). Focusing on Route 45 in particular (Routes 12 and 20 turn east at 95th Street), follow Route 45 south 5.5 miles. Immediately after crossing a short bridge over the Calumet Sag Channel, turn right onto Route 83 northbound. Follow Route 83 (Calumet Sag Road) 0.2 mile, then turn left into the Swallow Cliff Toboggan Slide and Winter Sports Area.

WALK: From the parking lot, cross a pedestrian bridge over the toboggan chutes. At the far end of the bridge, turn left and follow the edge of the woods 80 yards to join a trail entering the forest. Just inside the woods, pass a trail intersecting from the right, then another intersecting from the left. With the slope rising toward the left, follow the wide bridle path along the bottom of the bluff. Continue straight past a parking area on the right and across 104th Avenue.

Follow the bridle path as it gradually climbs west of 104th Avenue, then snakes through the woods. At an intersection with another wide bridle path, turn left downhill. Continue as the trail winds, dips, and climbs through the woods. Pass a trail intersecting from the right. Eventually, cross back over 104th Avenue.

Pass a trail intersecting from the rear-right. Ignore minor side-trails, but at a major fork in the bridle path, fork left. At the next trail junction, turn left. Follow the trail to the top of the toboggan chutes and to stairs descending to the parking lot.

If you want to extend your walk, there is also a trail loop east of 96th Avenue (Route 45), as shown on the map.

8

INDIANA DUNES STATE PARK

Walking or ski touring — 5 miles (8 kilometers). Sand ridges rise nearly two hundred feet from the southern shore of Lake Michigan. Cross the high foredunes and follow the beach to the Big Blowout, then return through sheltered woods behind the dunes. During winter, do not walk on the shelf of ice that sometimes extends out from the shore over the water. Dogs are prohibited on the beach and must be leashed elsewhere in the park. An admission fee is charged. Open daily 7:00 A.M. to 11:00 P.M. during summer and 8:00 A.M. to 11:00 P.M. during winter. Closed on Christmas. Managed by the Indiana Department of Natural Resources. Telephone (219) 926-4520.

"THE PROVINCE OF ECOLOGY is to consider the mutual relations between plants and their environment," wrote Henry Chandler Cowles in an article summarizing his research, during the late 1890s, of the plant communities of the Indiana Dunes and other dune regions bordering Lake Michigan. Today ecologists include both plants and animals within their preveiw, but as a graduate student at the University of Chicago and later as a professor of botany there, Cowles focused on ways that plants show special adaptations to the physical and climatic properties of their sites. An outgrowth of Darwinism, this subject was at the forefront of botanical research and was already under investigation by some European botanists on whose work Cowles built.

When a modified version of Cowles' doctoral thesis was

serialized in 1899 in the *Botanical Gazette,* it attracted world-wide attention among botanists. Cowles went on to write other leading articles in the developing field of plant ecology, and in 1912 he presented in London a well-received paper on his fifteen years of study at the Indiana Dunes. The following year, when Cowles organized the International Phytogeographic [plant geography] Excursion to America, all of the visiting European botanists put the Indiana Dunes — along with the Grand Canyon, Yosemite, and Yellowstone — on their list of places that they most wanted to see.

Cowles regarded the Indiana Dunes as a living laboratory ideally suited to ecological studies. "Plant formations should be found which are rapidly passing into other types by reason of a changing environment," he wrote, and pointed out that no land form is more changeable than a sand dune. Accordingly, he examined not only the features that enable some plants to survive and thrive where others fail, but also the dynamic rise and fall of distinct plant communities as their physical surroundings change — for example, as sand dunes grow or deteriorate or advance inland. Stressing the mutuality of the relationship between plants and their environment, he studied how plants themselves contribute to changes in local topography, soil, and other conditions, and how these modified conditions favor the rise to dominance of yet entirely different plant communities than were formerly present. This displacement of one biotic community by another is called *ecological succession,* and as Cowles pointed out, it can continue through several stages until change becomes so slow — depending, perhaps, on shifts in the climate itself — that a virtual equilibrium is achieved between the physical environment and the climax community of plants and animals.

One of Cowles' favorite pedagogical exercises was to conduct visitors and students through a succession of plant communities, starting at the bare beach and ending in the mature deciduous forest of the backdunes. This sequence in space is a metaphor for sequence in time; by walking inland the visitor

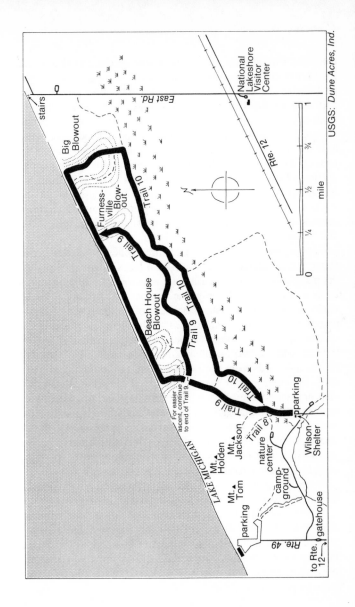

LAKE MICHIGAN

parking

Mt. Tom ▲

Mt. Holden ▲

Mt. Jackson ▲

nature center

campground

gatehouse

Rte. 49

to Rte. 12

Wilson Shelter

Trail 8

parking

Trail 9

Trail 10

Trail 10

Trail 9

Trail 9

Trail 10

For easier ascent, continue to end of Trail 9.

Beach House Blowout

Furnessville Blowout

Big Blowout

stairs

East Rd.

National Lakeshore Visitor Center

Rte. 12

N

0   ¼   ½   ¾   1

mile

USGS: *Dune Acres, Ind.*

can pass through stages of ecological succession that in all likelihood occurred in the backdunes at various times in the past. After all, the forested backdunes once were vacant beach and then grassy foredunes before they became far removed from the lake by a dramatic drop in water level. This is not to say that the present-day beach eventually will become forest also — at least, not in the absence of another big drop in the level of the lake. (See Chapter 7 for a discussion of the various levels of Lake Michigan.) In any case, as you walk from the beach through the dunes and down into the woods, notice the shifts in vegetation that correspond to the changing environmental factors of light intensity, temperature, wind, soil, water, and topography.

Cowles divided the beach into three zones: the lower beach that is washed by summer waves and lacks established plants; the middle beach that is washed by winter storms and inhabited by plants that live for only one season; and the upper beach where dune formation starts because of the presence of hardy perennial plants. Beginning, then, with the annual plants of the middle beach, one common species is sea rocket, a succulent (that is, water-filled) member of the mustard family. Although only a few yards from the water's edge, the middle beach is a very dry environment because of the glaring sun, the nearly constant wind warmed by the heated sand, and the porosity of the sand itself, through which rainwater quickly percolates. Accordingly, sea rocket shows several adaptations to its dry environment: fleshy stems and leaves that store water, a glossy leaf surface that helps to retain moisture, and disproportionately long, bushy roots to reach the water table.

Other pioneer plants of the middle beach are bugseed, winged pigweed, and seaside spurge. Bugseed is stiff with many branches and plump, narrow leaves that expose minimal surface to the sun. Similarly, winged pigweed has narrow, pointed leaves that resemble miniature holly. Seaside spurge has tiny leaves and hides from the wind by growing flat along the sand in a spreading mat; a large supply of latex in its leaves helps to preserve moisture.

Dune formation starts at the upper beach where, safe from winter storms, perennial plants establish a firm hold. The perennials form a living barrier that catches wind-blown sand to form small mounds that swell into foredunes as the vegetation spreads. Chief among the dune-building plants is marram grass, growing in dense clumps and tufts. Although marram grass produces a seed head each fall, the plant spreads mainly by *rhisome propagation*. Pushing outward from each established plant, underground stems sprout new roots and shoots. The rhisomes from a single plant sometimes spread as far as twenty feet. Together the underground stems and dense roots of many plants form a tight matrix that binds the sand so that it resists erosion even by waves. As the dunes grow vertically, the marram grass simply grows with it, keeping pace with the surface by pushing up fresh leaves from the buried central stem — a process called *internodal elongation* because the stem lengthens itself as necessary between leaf nodes. Marram grass is thus ideally suited to thrive in the unstable dune environment; in fact, when the sand surface becomes stabilized, the plant shows a decline in vigor because the underground stems, which continue to grow upward, get too near the surface and dry out.

In the shelter behind the front rank of marram-grass dunes, other grasses appear, including little bluestem bunchgrass and sand reed. Little bluestem bunchgrass, so-named because of its bright blue joints, show some ability to adjust to a shifting surface by internodal elongation, but it lacks underground runners, and so can sprout only from seeds. Sand reed, on the other hand, spreads by underground runners but lacks the ability to elongate its stem. Also, the rhisomes of sand reed tend to dive deep for moisture rather than to grow parallel with the surface; this adaptation serves it well when the dune is eroding, but when sand is accumulating, sand reed sometimes suffocates. As the buried grass decomposes, it provides nutrients for other plants and even trees, including the pioneering cottonwoods.

Frequently seen along the foredunes and sandy slopes fronting the lake, cottonwoods have wide, almost triangular, coarsely-toothed leaves. Like marram grass, these trees are major dune-builders because they can adjust to the changing sand surface. Cottonwood seeds require a sheltered, damp depression in which to sprout, but once the young trees are established, their foliage creates a windbreak that results in the deposition of drifting sand. Engulfment by sand would kill most trees, but cottonwoods can tolerate being buried. As the sand piles up and the water table rises within the growing dune, cottonwoods avoid suffocation by sprouting adventitious roots from successively higher levels of their trunks and branches. In this way, cottonwoods keep pace with a growing dune of their own making. What looks like stubby brush atop a dune may actually be the tip of a century-old, fifty-foot tree, as is sometimes plainly seen when the sand is blown away again, exposing a cottonwood that has a truck and branches shaggy with roots. These exposed roots can, in turn, form stems and sprout leaves. Cottonwood dunes tend to have steeper sides than marram-grass dunes because cottonwoods cannot spread sideways by underground runners, nor will their seeds sprout in the dry dune sand.

Other successful dune plants are two shrubs: sand-dune willow, with thick, small leaves adapted to the dry environment, and sand cherry, with reddish bark, narrow leathery leaves that turn bright red in the fall, and fruit that grows one to each stem. Both shrubs frequently are found behind the front rank of marram-grass dunes. Like cottonwood, sand-dune willow can sprout adventitious roots and can tolerate being buried and unburied. Like marram grass, sand cherry spreads by underground runners. Studies of sand cherry indicate that the roots of its seedlings tend to follow organic matter left by the burial of dune grasses.

The farther you walk into the foredunes, the greater becomes the variety of plants, including wormwood, wild rye, sand thistle, sand cress, goldenrod, milkweed, red osier dogwood, fragrant sumac, poison ivy, grapes, and many other plants, shrubs, and scrubby trees that are not unique to the dune region. One surprising plant, however, is the prickly-pear cactus, with round fat pads. Abundant in the desert regions of the Southwest, the cactus finds a similarly appropriate niche in the dry, sandy wastes of the dunes.

Along much of the lakeshore at the Indiana Dunes, the transition from the grassy, scrubby foredunes to the forested backdunes is fairly abrupt, since the mature woods often start immediately atop or behind the ridgeline of high dunes fronting the lake. But at the various blowouts along the shore, the transition is more confused and complex. Blowouts are places where the wind has breached the barrier of foredunes; channeled through a narrow gap, the wind then scours out a huge, amphitheater-like bowl. The high dunes are pushed back in a horseshoe-shaped bulge, and established forests are buried by the advancing dunes. Eventually the blowout becomes so big that the concentrated effect of the wind is dissipated, and the blowout is stabilized by vegetation.

As plants colonize the blowout, most of its low, uneven center is covered by the same species seen on the foredunes, including grasses, cottonwood, willow, and sand cherry. In the hollows at the center of the blowout, organic debris from decaying plants accumulates more quickly than elsewhere, and a few oaks may grow here from acorns dropped by chipmunks and squirrels. From the ridges adjacent to the blowout, evergreens such as juniper, jack pine, and perhaps even white pine spread downward into the blowout bowl. More striking than the living trees, however, are the dead ones in the so-called tree graveyards. Often still standing, these gray, dried relics show where forests were buried by the advancing dunes and then uncovered as the dunes moved onward. Sometimes a dark line across the sandy slope indicates a stratum of humus from which the former forest grew.

As just noted, at the top of the high dunes is a zone that often is occupied by a community of evergreens: juniper (both the slender, vertical red cedar and the low, spreading common

juniper), jack pine (with stiff, short needles, two to each fascicle), white pine (five long, soft needles to each fascicle), and bearberry (with papery, reddish stems and small, paddle-shaped leaves). These are among the first trees and shrubs after cottonwoods to become established on the windward slopes and crests of the high dunes near the lake, and they often are seen strung out in a long, narrow band that forms a buffer sheltering the deciduous forest of the backdunes. The evergreens sometimes occur on the backdunes as well, but the dense shade cast by the deciduous trees makes it very difficult for juniper and pine seedlings to compete successfully. The trees of the deciduous forest, however, cannot tolerate exposure to the wind, cold, and dryness of the high front dunes, and so there the evergreens find a niche for themselves.

The jack pines at the Indiana Dunes are an isolated colony located more than sixty miles south of any other stand of jack pine in the Great Lakes region. They are present here as a relic of the glacial period, when the climate of the entire Midwest, particulary near the ice sheet, was colder than at present. At the end of the Ice Age, most northern plants retreated with the glacier, but at the Indiana Dunes the jack pines remain because environmental conditions — particularly the meager soil, exposure to driving wind, and lack of water — in many ways resemble conditions farther north, where water is abundant but frequently unavailable because it is frozen as ice. The jack pine is so well adapted to the cold and physiological drought experienced by plants in the windy, ice-bound taiga that its range extends farther north into Canada than any other pine. Transpiration is minimized and resistence to cold is maximized by its short needles that have a cuticle so thick that it forms half the bulk of the leaf. Jack pines have singularly low nutritional requirements, and so can grow in dune sand, with its negligible content of humus.

Associated with the jack pine is bearberry, another plant common in Arctic regions. Bearberry is a low, woody creeper of the heath family, and once established, it provides cover that protects the young pines — which, of course, must grow from seeds — until they are big enough to survive on their own. Like marram grass, bearberry spreads by sending up new shoots from underground runners. Its growth, however, is slow; while it can adjust to some instability of the dune surface, it cannot survive a rapid accumulation of sand.

Sheltered from the wind by the high front dunes, the region to the rear is a suitable environment for a deciduous forest of oak, hickory, ash, maple, and other trees and shrubs that are not required to show any special tolerance to the shifting topography, drought, cold, or sterile soil that characterize the dunes nearer the lake. Here the terrain has been stabilized by vegetation that over the centuries has produced sufficient leaf litter and humus to support a rich and diversified forest. The various plant communities of the deciduous forest show only the usual differences between damp hollows, dry hilltops, north and south slopes, and other such conditions.

Of course, all is not static. Where the high front dunes are moving inland because of blowouts, the deciduous forest will simply be buried until the steep lee slopes of the advancing dunes are captured by grass, cottonwood, willow, cherry, and other dune-stabilizing plants. But absent an incursion by a migrating dune, the deciduous forest is the dominant plant complex among the backdunes, as it is throughout the Chicago region.

AUTOMOBILE: The Indiana Dunes are located at the southern end of Lake Michigan east of Gary. Route 12 runs parallel with the lakefront and provides access to the shore at various points. Route 12, in turn, can be reached via Interstate 90 or Interstate 94.

From the Dan Ryan Expressway southbound in Chicago, take Interstate 90 (the Skyway) east toward the Indiana Toll Road. South of Gary, leave I-90 at the exit for Routes 65, 12, and 20. Fork left for Routes 12 and 20 where Route 65 splits off to the right. Follow Routes 12 and 20 east 1 mile, then fork left for Route 12. Continue east on Route 12 for 8.8 miles to the exit for Route 49 on the right. From the top of the ramp, turn left and follow Route 49 north 0.9 mile to the entrance to Indiana Dunes State Park. From the gatehouse go 0.1 mile, then turn right toward the nature preserve. Follow the park road for 0.8 mile, then turn left into the parking lot next to the Wilson Shelter.

Another approach from Chicago is via Interstate 94 (the Dan Ryan Expressway, then the Calumet Expressway) toward Indiana. Stay on I-94 past the exit for the Skyway. Continue as I-94 merges with Interstate 80 eastbound toward Indiana. Later, stay on I-94 past the exit for Interstate 80 and Interstate 90 (Indiana Toll Road). Follow I-94 to the exit for Route 49 north toward the Indiana Dunes Recreation Area. Go north on Route 49 for 2.6 miles to the entrance to Indiana Dunes State Park. From the gatehouse go 0.1 mile, then turn right toward the nature preserve. Follow the park road for 0.8 mile, then turn left into the parking lot next to the Wilson Shelter.

Finally, from the suburbs north and west of Chicago, the dunes can be reached simply by following the Tri-State Tollway around Chicago toward Indiana. Eventually, the tollway joins Interstate 80 and Interstate 94 eastbound toward Indiana. Later, stay on I-94 past the exit for Interstate 80 and Interstate 90 (Indiana Toll Road). Follow I-94 to the exit for Route 49 north toward the Indiana Dunes Recreation Area. Go north on Route 49 for 2.6 miles to the entrance to Indiana Dunes State Park. From the gatehouse go 0.1 mile, then turn right toward the nature preserve. Follow the park road for 0.8 mile, then turn left into the parking lot next to the Wilson Shelter.

WALK: The trail starts to the left of an eight-foot-high boulder. Follow the path into the woods and across a bridge over a swamp. About 50 yards beyond the bridge, fork right onto Trails 9 and 10 (where Trail 8 forks left uphill). Go 150 yards, then fork left onto Trail 9. After 95 more yards, fork right to stay on Trail 9.

Follow Trail 9 up and down through the woods, at one point passing a path intersecting from Trail 10 on the right. Where Trail 9 turns eighty degrees to the right, fork left on a narrow path leading toward a high dune, visible through the woods straight ahead. Climb the wall of sand. (If, however, you would like an easier place to cross the dunes, continue on Trail 9 all the way to its end — about 1 mile — where the ascent is more gentle.)

From the crest of the dunes overlooking the lake, descend to the beach, then turn right along the shore. With the lake on the left, walk along the beach to the Big Blowout. And how, you ask, will you know which of the various gaps in the immense dunes near the shore is the Big Blowout? Here's how: If you crossed the dunes from Trail 9 as first recommended in the preceding paragraph, the Big Blowout is the third blowout along the shore. First you will pass the very conspicuous Beach House Blowout — a huge amphitheater-like formation open to the beach at a small, V-shaped cleft. Next, about three-quarters of a mile east of the Beach House Blowout, you will pass the far less conspicuous Furnessville Blowout. (If you took the easier route described in parentheses at the end of the preceding paragraph, you descended to the beach through Furnessville Blowout.) The Big Blowout is about a third of a mile east of Furnessville Blowout. Finally, if you reach a flight of stairs descending to the beach from a road near some houses, you have gone too far; retrace your steps along the beach about half a mile to the Big Blowout.

At the Big Blowout, climb the short bluff of sand at the back of the beach, then follow any of several footpaths leading inland through the irregular hummocks of the blowout. Notice occasional stumps and roots left from trees that formerly were buried by the advancing dunes but have since been uncovered. Climb to the crest of the dunes at the back of the blowout, then descend into the woods down a steep, sandy slope. At the bottom of the slope, turn right onto a footpath.

With the dunes toward the right, follow the path (Trail 10) through the woods. Eventually, bear left at a trail junction, then fork right at the next intersection. Continue through the woods, then bear left at another junction to stay on Trail 10. Immediately after Trail 9 intersects from the rear-right, fork left. Pass Trail 8 merging from the rear-right. Cross a bridge over a swamp, then emerge from the woods at the parking lot.

9

INDIANA DUNES NATIONAL LAKESHORE
West Beach

Walking or ski touring — 5 miles (8 kilometers). In a series of segments, this excursion passes through several different dune environments. After a walk along the beach, cross the high foredunes, then circle the flats where the sand has been strip mined. From a ridge overlooking Long Lake, return through the wooded hills and hollows of the backdunes. During winter, do not walk on the shelf of ice that sometimes extends out from the shore over the water. Dogs are prohibited in swimming areas and must be leashed elsewhere in the park. From May through September, an admission fee is charged. Open daily 9:00 A.M. until sunset. Managed by the National Park Service. Telephone (219) 926-7561.

THE INDIANA DUNES NATIONAL LAKESHORE was authorized by Congress in 1966, half a century after the idea was first reviewed at a public hearing held by the Department of the Interior. In 1916 the land under consideration was still virtually empty and untouched, stretching twenty-five miles from Gary to Michigan City. By the time the federal park actually was created, the area was a patchwork of steel mills, power plants, harbors, and residential developments strung out at intervals along the shore.

At first the impetus to preserve the Dunes came mainly from

Chicago, where rampant growth had produced, during the late nineteenth and early twentieth centuries, a countervailing movement for municipal parks and county forest preserves. Under the leadership of landscape architect Jens Jensen and other Chicago-based conservationists, the Indiana Dunes were identified as one of the nearby areas most worth keeping in their natural condition. In 1911 the conservationists organized the Prairie Club, which sponsored frequent excursions from Chicago to the Dunes via electric trolley and railroad. In 1914 the Prairie Club allied itself with other local organizations to form the Conservation Council of Chicago, and preservation of the Dunes became the council's first project. The council asked wealthy individuals and institutions to endow a Dunes arboretum and similar projects, but had no success. Nonetheless, the Conservation Council's persistent publicity campaign, which included illustrated lectures, guided hikes, and even theatrical productions in the Dunes, developed widespread support for preservation of the Dunes among Chicagoans and, to a lesser extent, among Indiana residents.

Opposition to a Dunes park was centered in Porter County, Indiana, where the main stretch of undeveloped Dunes land was located. This area was still a rural backwater, and local leaders and businessmen longed for industrial development. Despite local opposition, however, U.S. Senator Tom Taggart, whose political base was in central Indiana and who had pushed for the creation of municipal parks while mayor of Indianapolis, sponsored a Senate resolution in 1916 authorizing a study by the National Park Service of "the advisability of the securing by purchase or otherwise, all that portion of the counties of Lake, LaPorte, and Porter in the State of Indiana bordering on Lake Michigan and commonly known as the 'sand dunes' together with the cost of acquisition and maintenance."

Although seemingly straightforward, Taggart's proposal was out of the ordinary in several respects. At that time, Congress had never spent any money whatsoever to buy land for the

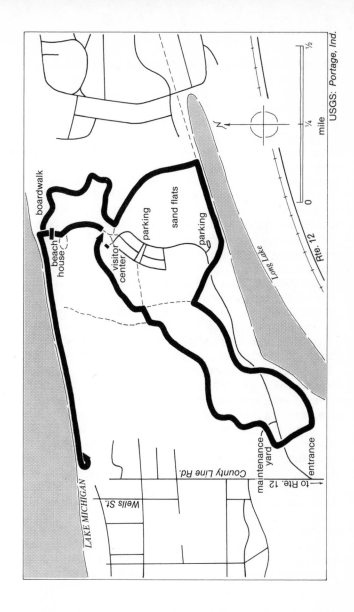

LAKE MICHIGAN

boardwalk

beach house

visitor center

parking

sand flats

parking

Long Lake

maintenance yard

entrance

County Line Rd.

Wells St.

to Rte. 12

Rte. 12

N

mile

0   1/4   1/2

USGS: Portage, Ind.

93

national parks; rather, the great national parks, starting with Yellowstone in 1872, had all been created from land already in federal ownership or donated by state governments. Also, the National Park Service, established by Congress in 1916 and under the direction of Chicagoan and Prairie Club member Stephen Mather, had formulated standards for the national parks to which the Indian Dunes did not conform. National parks were supposed to be monumental examples of natural grandeur. Park policy called for immense, pristine areas far removed from population centers — a policy that prevailed at the National Park Service until, nearly fifty years later, President John F. Kennedy and his Secretary of the Interior Stewart Udall initiated a new national park policy that stressed the development of smaller, recreation-oriented parks near large cities.

Although the Indiana Dunes were merely a sandbox compared to the existing national parks (all of which were in the West), Mather worked hard for a few months to support the Dunes park proposed by Senator Taggart's resolution and to prepare for a hearing on the matter. Held in Chicago, the hearing itself produced a lengthy litany of support for a park, although one witness cautioned that Congress "is singularly uninterested in national parks and there is no precedent for buying land for such a purpose." Disregarding precedent, Mather filed a report a month later endorsing federal purchase of twelve thousand acres of Dunes land at a cost of $2.6 million. The federal government, however, was preoccupied with America's entry into World War I, and Mather's report never received Congressional consideration. Moreover, Senator Taggart was defeated in his bid for re-election in the fall of 1916, and no Indiana politician took his place in support of a federal Dunes park.

Although Congress was indifferent to a Dunes national park, within a few years a much smaller park was created at the state level. In 1916 Indiana was one hundred years old, and the celebrations included the formation of a State Park Memorial

Committee to identify areas worthy of being preserved in commemoration of the state's centennial. Chairman and chief mover on the committee was Richard Lieber, a wealthy retired businessman turned conservationist. Lieber convinced the Indiana Federation of Women's Clubs and other local organiza-tions to appoint their own state park committees to solicit contributions to buy three state parks in the centennial year. Indiana's governor even declared a Park Contribution Week, and Lieber personally raised large sums from his wealthy friends. Altogether, however, only enough money was received to buy two state parks in central Indiana.

Indiana's first state parks proved to be immensely popular and established the precedent for still more state parks. Appointed state forester, Lieber persuaded the Indiana legislature to create a Department of Conservation in 1918, of which he was made director. In 1919 a state representative from Gary introduced a bill to establish the Indiana Dunes State Park. The bill produced no immediate result, but in 1920 construction of the Dunes Highway (present-day Route 12) added a sense of urgency that something must be done to protect the Dunes from the development that the road would surely bring. That same year the National Dunes Park Association — chief proponent of a federal preserve — went on record as supporting a state park instead.

In 1921 a bill to create a state park reached the floor of the Indiana legislature but failed to pass, in part because opponents in Porter County were unwilling to accept any park that included more than three miles of frontage on Lake Michigan instead of the nine miles suggested by the preservationists. Park advocates, led by Lieber and Bess Sheehan, chairman of the Dunes Park Committee of the State Federated Woman's Club, spent 1922 gathering public support for a Dunes park. Meanwhile, incursions in the Dunes continued as the residential communities of Dune Acres and Ogden Dunes were developed. In 1923 legislation to create a Dunes state park was again introduced, and after intense lobbying by its supporters, a three-mile park was approved on the last day of the legislative session. To implement the legislation, Lieber struggled to augment the $105,000 annual appropriation with private contributions, and he succeeded in raising several hundred thousand dollars from wealthy philanthropists, including Julius Rosenwald, president of Sears, Roebuck & Company, and Judge Elbert Gary, chairman of the board of U.S. Steel. By 1927 the state completed purchasing the two thousand acres that comprise the Indiana Dunes State Park.

Creation of the state park ended, for more than twenty years, all effort to establish a larger federal park in the Indiana Dunes. The issue lay dormant because for decades there was no industrial expansion into the Dunes. First the Great Depression intervened, then World War II. During this period 3,600 acres of spectacular duneland fronting the beach between the communities of Ogden Dunes in the west and Dune Acres in the east — a section called the Central Dunes — remained unchanged and apparently unthreatened. But after the war the Midwest boomed and became a tremendous market for steel, principally for use in automobiles and large appliances. In 1956 the Bethlehem Steel Company began quietly to buy large holdings in the Central Dunes from land speculation companies that had held the property since the early 1900s, and in 1962 Bethlehem announced plans to build a billion-dollar, fully integrated steel works on its newly-acquired land.

Bethlehem's plans were contingent on the development of a publicly-financed harbor at Burns Ditch, a small waterway that had been carved through the Dunes when the Little Calumet River had been relocated in 1926. Ever since the construction of Burns Ditch, big business in northern Indiana had dreamed of a major public port to stimulate industrialization and farm exports, and the project had gained plausibility after work began in 1955 on the St. Lawrence Seaway, which promised direct shipping access to the word. In 1957 Bethlehem gave the State of Indiana's Board of Public Harbors and Terminals a purchase option for 260 acres of waterfront duneland. Enthralled at the prospect of a major port, Indiana officials foresaw "7,000 three-year jobs for the building trades; 15,000 direct jobs in the steel mills; 25,000 jobs in service, allied industries, transportation and miscellaneous occupations; $2 billion in home and industry construction; and federal condemnation costs of $50 million" — if, that is, the Army Corps of Engineers would approve the harbor and the federal government pay for it. According to the cost-benefit studies conducted by the Corps of Engineers, the feasibility of a port depended on its heavy use by a major Bethlehem mill, but Bethlehem would not promise to build such a plant until a publicly-financed port was a certainty. Among Indiana, the federal government, and Bethlehem Steel, each wanted the others to demonstrate their commitment by building first.

Meanwhile, Bethlehem's land acquisitions had sparked a renewed effort to save the Central Dunes for a national park. The same factors that made the site attractive to Bethlehem — its large size, lake frontage, and lack of development — also made the area the most suited section of duneland for preservation. Moreover, by the early 1960s there was precedent for the National Park Service to buy waterfront areas. The Cape Hatteras National Seashore (paid for by the Mellon family) had been established in 1937, and in 1961, at the urging of the new Kennedy administration, Congress had authorized the Cape Cod National Seashore, the first national park to be acquired with Congressionally appropriated funds.

Indiana politicians at the local, state, and national levels were overwhelmingly behind the proposal for a harbor and steel mill, so park advocates had to look out-of-state for a spokesman to lead their crusade in Congress. In 1957 the Save the Dunes Council, which had been trying for five years to raise private funds to buy duneland, enlisted the aid of Illinois Senator Paul Douglas, who had a weekend house in the Dunes. Douglas tried to persuade Indiana's senators to sponsor park legislation, but they declined, and so in 1958 Douglas introduced the first of a long series of bills designed to protect and preserve the still unspoiled Central Dunes in Porter County.

Douglas's first proposal called for a federal reservation of nearly four thousand acres with 3½ miles of shoreline, including the land targeted by Indiana for a port and the land purchased by Bethlehem Steel. The Indiana press, politicians, and industrial spokesmen responded with outrage, accusing Douglas of carpetbagging, of trying to be the "third senator from Indiana," of representing Chicago commercial interests that sought to prevent Indiana's industrial development, and of wanting a park outside Illinois to be patronized by blacks from Chicago's South Side. Douglas' first bill never even received a hearing from the Senate committee responsible for national parks, but Douglas and the Save the Dunes Council, under the leadership of clubwoman Dorothy Buell (who followed in the footsteps of Bess Sheehan) continued to amass popular support for a national lakeshore park.

Soon, however, a series of major projects got underway in the Dunes, and together these works spelled the end of a Dunes national park as Douglas and others had at first envisioned it. In 1959 Bethlehem Steel swapped some of its land with the Northern Indiana Public Service Company in order to enable NIPSCO to build a $30 million coal-fired power station that would supply electricity to the proposed Burns Harbor Steel Mill. At the same time that construction began on the NIPSCO plant, the Midwest Steel Company, which owned land to the west of Bethlehem, started work on a $100-million finishing plant. Although a port was not essential to the Midwest plant, Midwest wanted a port and could be counted as among potential users whose business would help to justify port construction. In 1960 Midwest and Bethlehem agreed jointly to contribute $4.5 million to Indiana to help pay for part of the port's installations. Then, in a decision termed by one observer as a "crucial and Machiavellian" maneuver, Bethlehem Steel moved to destroy the Central Dunes for park use while still not committing itself to build a steel mill: in 1961 Bethlehem announced that it had contracted to sell 2.5 million cubic yards of sand to Northwestern University to be used as fill for the expansion of Northwestern's campus into Lake Michigan. The sand would be taken from the proposed harbor site, which was soon sold to the State of Indiana. Actual sand mining began in April 1962, and when it was completed, Indiana undertook to start construction of a harbor, which at long last had been approved by the Corps of Engineers after repeated hearings and re-hearings called to address the objections of the port's opponents.

Finally, in December 1962, after Senator-elect Birch Bayh promised that he would support proposals for a federally-funded port, Bethlehem Steel announced plans to begin construction of its steel mill as soon as possible. By July 1963, giant earthmovers were leveling the Central Dunes to create an immense plateau fourteen feet above lake level. By 1965 Bethlehem had a finishing mill in operation, and in 1969 Bethlehem's integrated plant became a reality when the first coke oven began operation.

Construction of the Bethlehem plant and Burns Harbor broke the stalemate by which the steel company and the park advocates both vied to determine the fate of the Central Dunes. Defeated, the park proponents turned their attention elsewhere. As early as 1961, Indiana's Senator Vance Hartke had introduced a bill which proposed a park of six thousand acres, entirely excluding the Central Dunes, but the park partisans had attacked Hartke's proposal as a sellout to industry. By mid-1963, however, the Central Dunes had been flattened, and the Kennedy administration, which had been subjected to fierce lobbying from advocates for both a park and a port, announced a quintessential political compromise. At the president's request, the Bureau of the Budget recommended federal funding for the Burns Harbor and also for an 11,700-acre Dunes park.

Two years later, on October 27, 1965, Congress passed a public works bill that included the Burns Harbor project, but a proviso stipulated that no funds would be appropriated for the harbor until both Houses of Congress had voted on the proposed Indiana Dunes National Lakeshore. A year later, on

October 14, 1966, Congress authorized a 6,539-acre federal park containing no land in common with the original Douglas proposal, having 5,161 acres less than that recommended by the Kennedy compromise three years earlier, and split into two main sections separated by a huge industrial complex.

Since Congressional approval in 1966, plans for the Indiana Dunes National Lakeshore have been slowly implemented and expanded. Six years passed before the National Park Service judged that it had purchased enough land to establish the park formally. Secretary of the Interior Walter Hickel under President Nixon continued the Kennedy/Udall policy of developing small, recreation-oriented national parks near large cities, but after Hickel resigned in protest against the Vietnam War, the Nixon administration and subsequent presidents pulled back from the urban park concept, ostensibly to reduce budgets. Nonetheless, at the urging of Porter County's first Democratic representative in forty-two years, Congress voted to enlarge the Dunes lakeshore by 3,300 acres in 1976 and by 500 acres in 1980. On both occasions the expansion was voted over the opposition of the National Park Service, which thought that the land in question was too expensive. Indeed, during the tenure of James Watt as secretary of the interior during Ronald Reagan's first term, a serious effort was made within the Interior Department to disestablish and eliminate the lakeshore park altogether. Watt called the new urban national parks "merely minor playgrounds" that never should have been authorized in the first place. Although de-authorization was thwarted, land acquisition at the Indiana Dunes slowed still further as Watt held back funds and curtailed condemnation proceedings. However, Watt's campaign against the dunes lakeshore proved to be entirely out of step with popular sentiment supporting the park. After Watt resigned under the pressure of nationwide reaction against his anti-park, anti-conservation policies, funds were made available to complete authorized acquisitions at the dunes lakeshore, and in 1986 Congress authorized the acquisition of yet another 853 acres.

And now for a straight editorial pitch. In the course of writing my various Country Walks books, I have seen a great many parks serving some of the nation's largest cities (which, of course, are going to get larger — very much larger — during the coming centuries). With its lake frontage, mountainous sand dunes, swamps, and wooded hollows, the Indiana Dunes are unsurpassed for scenic and recreational value. In the next century and beyond, the survival of the Dunes as public parkland will seem a miracle: a godsend to millions of people. So after your visit, if you think that the national lakeshore is worth preserving and expanding, write to your Congressperson and send copies of your letter to the representatives from Indiana's first and second congressional districts. Tell your representative that funds should be made available to complete authorized acquisitions, that further acquisitions to create more coherent boundaries should be authorized, and that residential inholdings should be eliminated.

AUTOMOBILE: The Indiana Dunes are located at the southern end of Lake Michigan east of Gary. Route 12 runs parallel with the lakefront and provides access to the shore at various points. Route 12, in turn, can be reached via Interstate 90 or Interstate 94.

From the Dan Ryan Expressway southbound in Chicago, take Interstate 90 (the Skyway) east toward the Indiana Toll Road. South of Gary, leave I-90 at the exit for Routes 65, 12, and 20. Fork left for Routes 12 and 20 where Route 65 splits off to the right. Follow Routes 12 and 20 east 1 mile, then fork left for Route 12. Continue east on Route 12 for 3.3 miles, then turn left onto County Line Road toward Indiana Dunes National Lakeshore — West Beach. Go 0.1 mile across a railroad, then fork right to enter the park. Follow the entrance road 1.3 miles to the large parking lot by the visitor center.

Another approach from Chicago is via Interstate 94 (the Dan Ryan Expressway, then the Calumet Expressway) toward Indiana. Stay on I-94 past the exit for the Skyway. Continue as I-94 merges with Interstate 80 eastbound toward Indiana. Later, stay on I-94 past the exit for Interstate 80 and Interstate 90 (Indiana Toll Road). Follow I-94 to the exit for Route 249 (Port of Indiana). From the top of the exit ramp off I-94, follow Route 249 north 1.8 miles to the exit for Route 12 (Michigan City). At the bottom of the exit ramp off Route 249, turn left (west) onto Route 12 toward Gary. Go 3.7 miles, then turn right onto County Line Road toward Indiana Dunes National Lakeshore — West Beach. Cross the railroad, then fork right into the park.

Finally, from the suburbs north and west of Chicago, the dunes can be reached simply by following the Tri-State Tollway around Chicago toward Indiana. Eventually, the tollway joins Interstate 80 and Interstate 94 eastbound toward Indiana. Later, stay on I-94 past the exit for Interstate 80 and Interstate 90 (Indiana Toll Road). Follow I-94 to the exit for Route 249 (Port of Indiana). From the top of the exit ramp off I-94, follow Route 249 north 1.8 miles to the exit for Route 12 (Michigan City). At the bottom of the exit ramp off Route 249, turn left (west) onto Route 12 toward Gary. Go 3.7 miles, then turn right onto County Line Road toward Indiana Dunes National Lakeshore — West Beach. Cross the railroad, then fork right into the park.

WALK: From the end of the parking lot nearest the beach, follow a wide asphalt drive to the beach house and lakeshore.

For a walk along the beach, turn left. With the lake on the right, follow the beach 0.8 mile to the Wills Street Beach (or farther if you want), then return to the beach house.

For a walk through the dunes and sand flats inland from

the lake, join a boardwalk at the head of the beach-house stairs. With the lake on the left, follow the boardwalk up and over the dunes, then to the right inland and over still larger dunes. Descend toward the parking lot. At the bottom of the slope, turn left to continue on the circuit shown on the map.

With the dunes on the left, follow the bottom of the slope through a large area where the sand has been strip mined. Bear right at a trail junction in front of a shallow slough called Long Lake. With Long Lake on the left, head west on the level path leading past a parking lot on the right, then across the entrance road. Continue across the flats, then turn left at a trail intersection. Follow an old railroad bed formerly used when the sand was removed. Cross back over the entrance road. Follow the path to the top of a ridge overlooking Long Lake.

With Long Lake toward the left, continue on the path along the ridge. Eventually, follow the trail to the right downhill, through scrubby woods, and across the entrance road for the third time. Turn right in front of a fence enclosing the park maintenance yard, then cross a driveway. Continue as the trail climbs, dips, and winds through wooded dunes. Eventually, within sight of the lake, descend steeply, then turn left as the trail heads toward the foredunes to complete the circuit.

10

INDIANA DUNES NATIONAL LAKESHORE
Mount Baldy

Walking — up to 4 miles (6.4 kilometers), depending on the condition of the beach west of Mount Baldy. Because of high water and ongoing erosion, conditions along the shore change annually, and so the beach may be impassable at some places and at some times. In any case, explore the Saharan plateau atop Mount Baldy (which in itself is worth a visit), then follow the narrow beach for as far as it is passable. Return by the way you came. Because the beach is very narrow, a walk here may entail wet feet. During winter, do not walk on the shelf of ice that sometimes extends out from the bluff over the water. Dogs must be leashed. Open daily from 6:00 A.M. to 8:00 P.M. Managed by the National Park Service. Telephone (219) 926-7561.

MOUNT BALDY is on the move. Rising abruptly from the water at the eastern end of the national lakeshore, this huge, bare hill of sand is advancing inland at a rate of four or five feet per year, burying everything in its path. When a strong wind blows off the lake, the entire front surface of the dune is swept by a blast of sand scudding up the steep slope in a gritty, stinging blizzard. Blowing over the crest of the dune, which at Mount Baldy is more than 120 feet high, the flying sand resembles a swirling plume of smoke that quickly dissipates as

the sand falls down the sharp lee slope and rains on the woods beyond. The leaves of black oaks at the foot of the slope turn brown in midsummer as the sand rises around the trunks and the trees die.

Mount Baldy is not the only major duneland feature that is moving; for two or three miles to the southwest of Mount Baldy, the entire shoreline is receding. Here the beach is very narrow, and waves lap at the foot of the dunes, forming a steep sand bluff that slumps into the lake with each storm, sometimes bringing down trees and even houses that were perched at the top.

There are two main reasons for the rampant erosion seen in the vicinity of Mount Baldy. The first is simply high water. As of 1986, the Great Lakes were at the highest level ever noted during the 120 years that records have been kept. Most experts attribute the rising water to a twenty-year period of unusually great precipitation, and they predict that the water will remain high — and perhaps continue to rise — for years to come. Some public officials and organizations representing lakefront communities even have suggested that the Niagara River be enlarged to drain off excess water from the Great Lakes.

High water is a problem, but obviously it does not entirely account for the severe erosion that is occurring at some areas along the shore — at Mount Baldy, for example — but not at other places. Rather, the erosion at Mount Baldy is in part traceable to human action. In Lake Michigan the prevailing current along both the eastern and western shores is southward, with the result that over a period of ten thousand years immense quantities of sand have been conveyed to the southern tip of the lake to form the dunes at the Indiana shore. This process, of course, is ongoing, and at any given point along the shore, the continuing influx of sand from the north replaces what is washed southward or blown inland. In some places, however, harbor projects and other lakefront developments have altered the equation locally. For example, 1½ miles northeast along the lakefront from Mount Baldy, the longshore current has

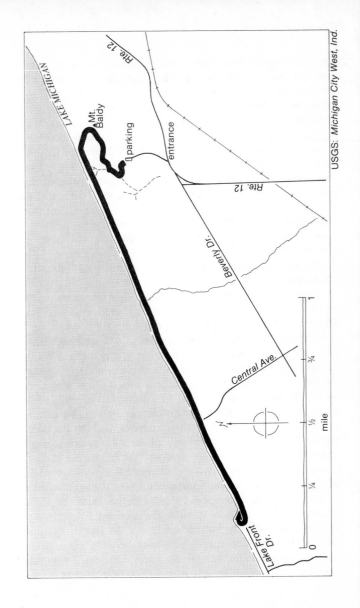

LAKE MICHIGAN

Rte. 12

Mt. Baldy

parking

entrance

Rte. 12

Beverly Dr.

Central Ave.

N

Lake Front Dr.

0   ¼   ½   ¾   1

mile

USGS: Michigan City West, Ind.

107

been interrupted by a massive jetty projecting more than three hundred yards into the lake at Michigan City. Built to protect boats in the Michigan City harbor and to prevent sand from filling in the harbor channel, the jetty has disrupted the longshore current, causing sand to accumulate on the upcurrent (or northeast) side of the projection, where a very wide beach has formed. But the deposition of sand above Michigan City has produced a corresponding imbalance downcurrent, where more sand is washed away by waves than arrives from upstream. The U.S. Army Corps of Engineers estimates that 60 percent of the erosion along the three miles of shoreline downcurrent from Michigan City is attributable to the harbor jetty. In an effort to save Mount Baldy from being consumed by the lake, the National Park Service in cooperation with the Corps of Engineers has dumped more than a million cubic yards of sand on the Mount Baldy beach.

Of course, some instability along the shore is normal. After all, the beach and dunes are the combined result of lake currents, waves, and wind that are not always constant or in equilibrium. As already noted, cycles of low and high water extending over a period of years have a major effect on the lakeshore. Even on a yearly basis, a cycle of change is apparent. Winter, for example, is usually a period of net loss along the beach. The strongest winds, blowing at forty or fifty miles per hour from the north and northwest, occur most often during winter. Large waves eat into the foredunes, and the backwash carries the eroded sand offshore, where it is reworked into a series of sandbars visible as shadows just below the surface. Conversely, the small waves that are typical of summer gradually push the sand ashore. Sometimes during the summer a bar forms just off the beach, then slowly merges with the shore. Because of the longshore current, the sand usually returns to the beach downcurrent from where it was last eroded from the land. In this manner, a rough balance between erosion and accretion maintains the beach indefinitely, although it may vary in width from season to season and from year to year.

Once on the beach, the sand is exposed to the wind. When the wind reaches seven miles per hour, the sand begins to move. At first it simply rolls along, but at higher wind velocities, the sand bounces across the surface in a process called *saltation*. When the wind reaches twenty miles per hour, the sand is picked up and carried through the air like dust, although usually not more than a few feet above the surface. Onshore winds move the sand inland, and gradually a sinuous foredune is produced running parallel with the water's edge and ranging in height from a few feet to 50, 75, or even 100 feet. As discussed in Chapter 8, the growth of foredunes is greatly affected by vegetation. Grass, shrubs, and trees form obstacles where the wind is slowed and sand is deposited. As vegetation spreads, the foredunes are stabilized.

Sometimes, however, a disturbance, such as wave erosion, fire, or tramping and treading by park visitors, kills the vegetation and enables the wind to blow away the loose sand. A gap develops in the foredunes, and as it grows bigger, the gap provides a channel through which the wind rushes, scouring out the sand on either side and blowing it to the rear over the crest of the dune, which thus begins to move. As the dune migrates inland, it fans out in a horseshoe-shaped bulge with its open end toward the lake. The result is a large, bare bowl called a *blowout*. At the back of the blowout, the sand that use to occupy the cavity may form a mound rising to unusual heights, as at 192-foot Mount Tom in the Indiana Dunes State Park. Eventually, the blowout becomes so large that the effect of the wind is dissipated, and the entire formation is once again stabilized by vegetation. In the front rank of dunes, however, what passes for stability can never be regarded as permanent, as a walk at Mount Baldy and along the shore to the southwest should convince anyone.

AUTOMOBILE: The Indiana Dunes are located at the southern end of Lake Michigan east of Gary. Route 12 runs parallel with the lakefront and provides access to the shore at various points. Route 12, in turn, can be reached via Interstate 90 or Interstate 94.

From the Dan Ryan Expressway southbound in Chicago, take Interstate 90 (the Skyway) east toward the Indiana Toll Road. South of Gary, leave I-90 at the exit for Routes 65, 12, and 20. Fork left for Routes 12 and 20 where Route 65 splits off to the right. Follow Routes 12 and 20 east 1 mile, then fork left for Route 12. Continue east on Route 12 for 20.5 miles to the entrance for the Mount Baldy area on the left. Go 0.1 mile to the parking lot.

Another approach from Chicago is via Interstate 94 (the Dan Ryan Expressway, then the Calumet Expressway) toward Indiana. Stay on I-94 past the exit for the Skyway. Continue as I-94 merges with Interstate 80 eastbound toward Indiana. Later, stay on I-94 past the exit for Interstate 80 and Interstate 90 (Indiana Toll Road). Follow I-94 to the exit for Route 49 north toward the Indiana Dunes Recreation Area. Go north on Route 49 for 1.7 miles to the turnoff — on the left — for Route 12 and the National Lakeshore. At the bottom of the ramp, turn right onto Route 12 and go 8.4 miles to the entrance for the Mount Baldy area on the left. Go 0.1 mile to the parking lot.

Finally, from the suburbs north and west of Chicago, the dunes can be reached simply by following the Tri-State Tollway around Chicago toward Indiana. Eventually, the tollway joins Interstate 80 and Interstate 94 eastbound toward Indiana. Later, stay on I-94 past the exit for Interstate 80 and Interstate 90 (Indiana Toll Road). Follow I-94 to the exit for Route 49 north toward the Indiana Dunes Recreation Area. Go north on Route 49 for 1.7 miles to the turnoff — on the left — for Route 12 and the National Lakeshore. At the bottom of the ramp, turn right onto Route 12 and go 8.4 miles to the entrance for the Mount Baldy area on the left. Go 0.1 mile to the parking lot.

WALK: From the back of the parking lot, follow the main path toward the beach. As the lake comes into sight, turn right at the crest of the dunes to explore the summit of Mount Baldy. Descend across the sandy slope to the beach. With the lake on the right, follow the narrow beach for as far as it is safely passable, then return by the way you came. Because of ongoing erosion, conditions here change annually, and so you must use good judgment to evaluate the circumstances that you find. But do not, please, climb on the sandy bluffs, since doing so contributes to erosion.

11

ILLINOIS AND MICHIGAN CANAL

Walking, bicycling, or ski touring — up to 15 miles (24.2 kilometers) one way. Hike from Channahon to Morris (or vice versa) along one of the most attractive sections of this historic commercial waterway. For 5 miles along the Kankakee Bluffs, the towpath overlooks the Des Plaines and Illinois Rivers, then cuts through woods and fields before again bordering the Illinois River at Morris. If you do not want to retrace your steps, a car shuttle is necessary. Aside from Channahon and Morris, two other access points are described under the automobile directions, making possible several shorter trips. Dogs must be leashed. Open daily from dawn until dusk. Managed by the Illinois Department of Conservation. Telephone (815) 942-0796.

COMPLETED IN 1848, the Illinois and Michigan Canal once stretched ninety-six miles from Chicago southwest along the valleys of the Des Plaines and Illinois Rivers to LaSalle, below which the Illinois River itself was navigable to the Mississippi. Today, some sections of the canal no longer exist; other stretches are dry and overgrown; but still other parts have been repaired and developed for walking, bicycling, and canoeing. As an introduction to the canal, the excursion described here focuses on the fifteen miles between Channahon and Morris, where the canal has been restored to the appearance of a nineteenth-century waterway for mule-drawn boats. Lift locks, locktenders' houses, aqueducts, and other intriguing works punctuate a walk along this section of the towpath,

which overlooks the Des Plaines and Illinois Rivers for much of its length.

The Illinois and Michigan Canal follows the river channel carved at the end of the last glacial period, when Lake Michigan drained to the southwest until withdrawal of the ice sheet uncovered a lower outlet to the north. During the time that the lake emptied to the southwest, the torrent cut downward through the moraines near Chicago until the elevation of the gap is now only a dozen feet higher than Lake Michigan. The low terrain separating the Chicago River (which has its mouth at Lake Michigan) and the Des Plaines River (which flows southwest to the Illinois River) became the Chicago Portage — a route used by Indians to transfer canoes between the lake and the Illinois River.

A canal at the Chicago Portage was proposed by the earliest European explorers. Guided by Indians, Louis Joliet and Father Jacques Marquette passed from the Illinois River to the Des Plaines to the South Branch of the Chicago River in 1673, after first having reached the Mississippi by way of the Wisconsin River. Joliet and Marquette had descended the Mississippi as far as the confluence with the Arkansas River and had satisfied themselves that the Mississippi emptied into the Gulf of Mexico. The official Jesuit report of their expedition states:

> According to the researches and explorations of Joliet, we can easily go to Florida in boats and by a very good navigation with slight improvements. There will be but one canal to make — and that by cutting only one half league of prairie from the lake of the Illinois [that is, Lake Michigan] into the St. Louis River [Illinois River], which empties into the Mississippi. . . .

Nine years later, Robert LaSalle also recommended construction of a canal linking Lake Michigan and the Illinois River after returning from his voyage all the way down the Mississippi to the Gulf of Mexico.

The French, however, never went to the expense of building a canal. Despite an official policy that favored agricultural

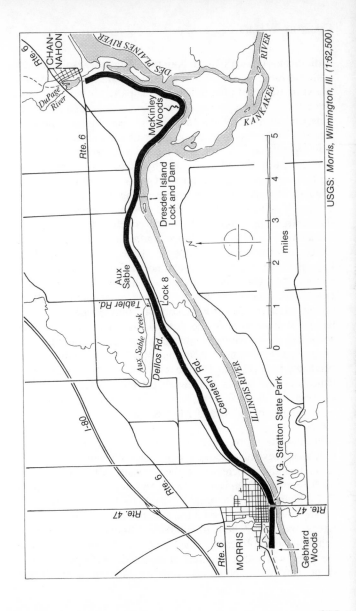

USGS: *Morris, Wilmington, Ill.* (1:62,500)

CHAN-
NAHON
Rte. 6
DES PLAINES RIVER
DuPage
River
Rte. 6
McKinley
Woods
KANKAKEE RIVER
Dresden Island
Lock and Dam
N
5
4
3
2 miles
1
0
Aux
Sable
Tabler Rd.
Lock 8
Aux Sable Creek
Dellos Rd.
Cemetery Rd.
ILLINOIS RIVER
I-80
Rte. 6
W. G. Stratton State Park
Rte. 47
Rte. 6
MORRIS
Gebhard
Woods

115

settlements, France's North American empire (which included both the Saint Lawrence and Mississippi watersheds) concentrated on trade with the Indians, principally for beaver pelts, a light cargo. This commerce was conducted through numerous independent trappers and traders who each winter fanned out into the wilderness to hunt and trap with the Indians. Transport was by bateaux — that is, simply large canoes. In consequence, a wagon road maintained by a few resident traders was all that was necessary to transport boats and cargo across the Chicago Portage and other such carrying points.

French rule in North America lasted only a hundred years. By the Treaty of Paris, which in 1763 concluded the French and Indian War, Great Britain gained control of Canada, the Great Lakes, and the territory east of the Mississippi. In spite of the large part that England's colonial population had played in the victory, the movement of settlers into the interior of the continent was thereafter prohibited instead of encouraged. By a proclamation in 1763, King George III forbade the granting or taking of land west of the Appalachian Mountains, where, according to one cabinet minister, the populace would be "out of reach of government." Not until the colonies gained independence in 1782 and Congress passed the Northwest Ordinance of 1787 was a framework established for the orderly settlement, development, and government of the region bounded by the Ohio and Mississippi Rivers and the Great Lakes.

During the following three decades leading up to Illinois statehood, several proposals were made by high federal officials, including Secretary of the Treasury Albert Gallatin in 1807, President Madison in 1814, and Secretary of War John C. Calhoun in 1819, to build a canal at the Chicago Portage. A canal, it was argued, would aid in the defense of the Great Lakes and would help to bind the Mississippi Valley economically and politically to the East Coast, but in each instance the plan was either ignored or rejected by Congress. The skepticism of Congressmen from the Atlantic states is not surprising; even in 1818, when Illinois was admitted to the Union, the population of the northern part of the state was virtually all Indian. White settlements in the new state of Illinois were concentrated along the Ohio and Mississippi Rivers, and even the state capital was at Kaskaskia, south of St. Louis. When agents from Illinois and Indiana met at Chicago in 1821 to survey the boundary between their states, they found (aside from the federal garrison at Fort Dearborn) a village lacking "any kind of civil government" and consisting of only nine or ten houses, all occupied by French traders and their families.

When Illinois became a state, however, proponents of a canal gained one important concession. The state's northern boundary, which as first proposed was a westward extension of the line separating Indiana and Michigan, was moved fifty miles north so that the Chicago Portage would be included in Illinois. During the early years of statehood, Representative Daniel P. Cook urged Congress to help Illinois build a publicly owned canal by giving the state federally owned land along the proposed route. (Under the Northwest Ordinance, the federal government had the power of "primary disposal" of all land to which title had been obtained from the Indians; in 1816 the land at the Chicago Portage had been ceded to the federal government by a treaty with the United Tribes of the Ottawa, Chippewa, and Potawatomi.) After some fumbling, the state received in 1827 a grant of land not only for the canal itself but also of every other square mile in a checkerboard swath five miles wide along the entire length of the proposed canal, provided the canal was begun in five years and completed in twenty. The cost of building the canal was supposed to be financed by selling the bordering land.

In 1829 the state appointed a Board of Canal Commissioners, and the next year a survey of the canal route was begun. In 1831, however, the state legislature instructed the commissioners to consider also an alternative proposal for a railroad. Construction of the first commercial railroad in Amer-

117

ica — the Baltimore and Ohio — had begun in Baltimore in 1828 and after only two years the railroad's progress west toward the Ohio River clearly was outstripping the competing — and far more costly — Chesapeake and Ohio Canal, on which work had started the same day. When the survey engineer hired by the Illinois canal commissioners submitted his final report in 1833, he strongly recommended building a railroad, which by various estimates would cost a quarter or a third as much as a canal. A railroad could also run year-around, while a canal would be forced to close in winter. At the request of the Illinois legislature, Congress authorized the state to use the land donated by the federal government for either a canal or a railroad, and also extended by five years the time limit to start construction, for the state still lacked the money to begin. Sale of the land had begun in 1830, but the proceeds were disappointing and clearly would not be enough to pay for a canal. Finally, in 1833 the state abolished the Board of Canal Commissioners and repealed all canal legislation.

For the next year Illinois debated what to do. The gubernatorial election of 1834 was run almost entirely on the issue of a canal versus a railroad, and the canal candidate won. The canal proponents had raised the specter of a private railroad monopoly charging prohibitive freight rates; the canal, in contrast, would be owned by the state. Canal advocates also argued that a canal could move extremely heavy, bulk loads better than a railroad. Most importantly, the Erie Canal, completed in 1825, was proving to be a great success. Already vessels arriving in Chicago had jumped from 12 in 1832 to 180 in 1834, when Chicago's harbor was improved at federal expense. Platted in 1830 and incorporated as a village in 1833, Chicago was a booming frontier town.

In 1835 the Illinois legislature appointed a new Board of Canal Commissioners, which secured a loan of $500,000 to begin work. The commissioners hired William Gooding as Chief Engineer to design the canal and to supervise its construction. They also decided that the canal should be built according to a "deep cut" plan by which the channel west from

Chicago would be dug so deep that the water of Lake Michigan would flow by gravity through the South Branch of the Chicago River directly into the canal and from there down the entire length of the canal to the Illinois River at LaSalle. In 1836 contractors began work on the canal itself.

Construction of the I & M Canal was plagued by financial problems. In 1839 the canal commissioners ran out of money, and the canal was on the brink of abandonment. Work continued into 1841 only because some contractors agreed to buy $1,200,000 worth of canal bonds. In 1842 the Illinois State Bank failed, and work on the canal stopped altogether while the state tried to borrow more money. The "deep cut" plan was dropped in favor of a far less expensive but more cumbersome "shallow cut" canal. In 1845 work on the canal resumed after a group of investors agreed to supply funds to finish the project, provided the canal was managed not by the state but by an independent board of three trustees, two of whom were selected by the investors. Finally, on April 20, 1848, the canal opened to navigation.

As completed, the canal was sixty feet wide at water level, thirty-six feet wide at the bottom, and six feet deep. It had eighteen locks. For boats traveling from east to west, the first two locks raised the boats to the summit level of the canal (to which water had to be pumped up from the Chicago River), and the rest of the locks controlled the gradual descent along the valleys of the Des Plaines and Illinois Rivers to LaSalle. The canal also featured four feeder canals to supply water to the main canal, and four aqueducts to carry the entire canal across various tributaries of the Illinois River. A different technique was used to cross the Des Plaines River at Joliet and the DuPage River at Channahon. In these cases each river was dammed to create a slackwater pool; boats left the canal on one side of the river, crossed through the slackwater pool, then re-entered the canal on the other side, as can be seen at Channahon immediately upstream from where the walk described below starts.

When the canal opened, it was mired in debt. It had cost

about four times the original estimate for a "shallow cut" canal; accrued interest on the backlog of unpaid checks, bonds, and loans swelled the total debt further. Moreover, the canal was on the verge of obsolescence. Already the railroads had demonstrated their superiority; by 1853 a railroad ran parallel with the canal, and by 1860 a number of railroads connected Chicago with the eastern seaboard. Nonetheless, under the management of the canal trustees, the waterway proved to be viable. Tolls not only covered annual operating expenses but also serviced the debt, which was entirely paid by 1871. The trustees then turned the canal and more than $95,000 in surplus funds over to the state.

Together with the railroads, the Illinois and Michigan Canal contributed substantially to the growth of Chicago and the other towns along the waterway. Grain, cattle, and hogs from points west were brought to Chicago by canal, making the city a major wheat market and meat-packing center. Building stone, coal, and sand were transported to the city from quarries and mines near the waterway. Lumber from the Great Lakes and merchandise from the eastern part of the country were shipped down the I & M to the burgeoning towns located along the canal and the Illinois River. Chicago was launched on its career as the great mid-continental shipping center. When the canal opened, the city's population was about 20,000. By 1850 the population was 28,269, and by 1854 it was 74,500. By 1855 more than half the population of Illinois lived north of Springfield (which had been made capital in 1837), and the most densely populated area was along the I & M Canal.

Because the locks of the I & M were the narrowest part of the entire canal and river system, boats using the waterway were made to fit the locks closely. Each lock was eighteen feet wide and 118 feet long, and the typical canal boat was not much smaller. On the Chicago and Illinois Rivers, the boats were towed by small steamers, but on the canal, each boat was pulled individually by a team of two to five horses or mules hitched to long towlines. Horses were faster, but mules were stronger and had more stamina. A team of three mules could haul a loaded boat at a steady pace of about two miles per hour in working shifts up to six hours long before being traded for a fresh team. A driver — frequently a boy as young as twelve or fourteen years — guided the team, either walking behind it or riding the rear animal. Other members of the crew were the helmsman, a bowman who handled the lines and used a stout pole to fend off obstructions and to maneuver through the locks, and the captain. Drivers, helmsmen, and bowmen were employed by the captain and paid set wages; each captain, in turn, was either an independent contractor for the freight company that owned the boat (in which case the captain received a share of the profits from each trip) or else he owned the boat himself (in which case he got the whole profit.)

The canal management operated no boats; its activities were confined to running the canal itself, for which it had several classes of employees. Most numerous were the locktenders, who lived in houses by the locks and were on call twenty-four hours a day to lock a boat through whenever it arrived. The procedure for locking entailed closing and opening the gates and valves in a set sequence. For example, after a boat heading down the canal had floated into the lock, the upstream gates were closed behind it and valves in the downstream gates were opened, draining the water into the canal below the lock and lowering the boat to that level. The valves were then closed, the downstream gates were opened, and the boat was towed out. For boats headed up the canal, the procedure was reversed; the water in the lock was raised by opening valves in the upstream gates after the boat was sealed in the lock. Alerted by the blast of a trumpet carried on each boat, the locktender would have the water at the right level and the appropriate gates opened for the approaching boat.

Other canal employees were the canal walkers, who were assigned to a section of the canal and inspected it every day. They maintained the canal at its proper level by adjusting the waste gates that allowed excess water to drain into streams. The towpath walkers also examined the locks and aqueducts for damage or signs of weakening, and checked the banks for erosion and burrowing animals. They noted items that needed attention, made temporary repairs as necessary, and in general tried to prevent small problems from becoming big ones.

Aside from the locktenders and the canal walkers, the I & M Canal had toll collectors stationed at Chicago, Lockport, and Ottawa. According to a complex schedule of rates, the toll depended on the type of cargo and its final destination. The collectors also supervised the locktenders and towpath walkers in their section of the canal, and were in turn supervised by the general superintendent whose office was at Lockport.

During the 1870s and '80s, traffic on the I & M Canal declined. In 1892 work began on the Chicago Sanitary and Ship Canal, which would be far larger than the I & M. By 1902 the Sanitary and Ship Canal extended from Chicago to Joliet, and traffic on the parallel section of the I & M virtually ended. Between Joliet and LaSalle, the old canal continued to be used, but in 1919 work began to channelize the Des Plaines and Illinois Rivers downstream from Joliet. When the Illinois Waterway opened in 1933, all of the Illinois and Michigan Canal was closed to navigation. Now from the towpath huge barges are often visible on the adjacent river system, which essentially is a larger canal with its own set of locks.

The recreational potential of the I & M Canal was recognized at the time of its closing. During the Depression the Civilian Conservation Corps renovated the towpath and built picnic areas and shelters along the former waterway. Even so, the canal deteriorated for forty years until 1974, when what was left was placed under the stewardship of the Illinois Department of Conservation. By then, however, parts of the canal were gone, most notably the eight miles nearest Chicago, which had been used as the right-of-way for the Stevenson Expressway. Other smaller sections had been transferred to local communities. Since 1974, however, local volunteers and the state have cleared long sections of the towpath and have repaired many original features of the canal. Aside from the fifteen miles between Channahon and Morris (described below), the towpath is also passable (although muddy in wet weather) west from Morris all the way to LaSalle; at some points detours are necessary. Other sections of the towpath will be cleared in the future.

AUTOMOBILE: The segment of the Illinois and Michigan Canal described here starts in Channahon, located 45 miles southwest of Chicago. Channahon is reached via Route 6 off Interstate 55.

From Chicago — or from the Tri-State Tollway southwest of Chicago — take Interstate 55 (Stevenson Expressway) south toward St. Louis. West of Joliet, pass the interchange with Interstate 80 (which provides a good approach from Gary and the suburbs south of Chicago). Leave I-55 at the exit for Route 6 toward Morris and the Illinois and Michigan Canal State Park.

From the top of the exit ramp off I-55, turn right onto Route 6. Go 2.2 miles, then turn left onto Center Street in Channahon (where North Street intersects from the right). Go 1 mile as Center Street curves right and turns into Bridge Street. Turn left into the parking lot for the I & M Canal State Trail, immediately after a bridge over the DuPage River but just before another bridge over the canal.

Three other access points — McKinley Woods, Aux Sable, and Gebhard Woods in Morris — are described below. If you do not want to retrace your steps, a car shuttle is necessary. Obviously, a shuttle involves either two cars and two driver-hikers, or a driver who simply meets you at the end. Another approach (one that I used) is to leave your car at Morris and there hire a taxi to drive you to the starting point in Channahon.

McKinley Woods is located 3 miles west along the towpath from the parking lot off Bridge Street in

Channahon. To reach McKinley Woods by car from the
Bridge Street parking lot, continue west on Bridge Street
0.7 mile, then turn left and go 2 miles to the entrance to
McKinley Woods, open from 8 A.M. to 8 P.M. in summer
and from 8 A.M. to 5 P.M. in winter. Follow the park road to
its end, descending steeply to the lower parking lot next to
the canal. A bridge located about 70 yards to the right of
a picnic pavilion leads to the towpath on the other side of
the canal.

Aux Sable at Lock 8 is located 8 miles west along the
towpath from the parking lot off Bridge Street in
Channahon. To reach Aux Sable by car from the Bridge
Street parking lot, follow Bridge Street west 0.8 mile to
Route 6. Continue west on Route 6 for 4.4 miles to a
crossroads with Tabler Road. Turn left onto Tabler Road
and go 1.4 miles, then turn right onto Dellos Road and go
0.2 mile to a parking lot at Aux Sable Access on the left.

Gebhard Woods in Morris is located 15 miles west
along the towpath from the parking lot off Bridge Street in
Channahon. To reach Gebhard Woods by car from the
Bridge Street parking lot, follow Bridge Street west 0.8
mile to Route 6. Continue west on Route 6 for 10.1 miles
to the intersection with Route 47 in Morris. Turn left onto
Route 47 and go 0.7 mile, then turn right onto Route 6
westbound. Go 0.5 mile, then turn left onto Union Street.
Go 0.6 mile to a T-intersection. Turn right onto Hazel
Street, then left onto Vine Street and continue to a T-
intersection with Fremont Avenue. Turn right and go 0.3
mile, then turn left onto Ottawa Street. Follow Ottawa
Street 0.2 mile, then turn left into Gebhard Woods.

WALK: From the parking lot off Bridge Street in
Channahon, follow the former towpath (now a gravel road)
with the canal on the right. Before long, the Des Plaines
River comes into sight on the left. Continue straight where

the gravel road turns left away from the canal. Eventually, pass a footbridge crossing the canal at McKinley Woods.

With the canal on the right, pass the confluence of the Des Plaines and Kankakee Rivers, which join to form the Illinois River. Pass Dresden Nuclear Power Station and Dresden Island Lock and Dam. Continue on the towpath — a dirt road sometimes used by automobiles — as the canal gradually slants right away from the Illinois River. At Cemetery Road, follow the path and canal under a road bridge. Continue with the canal on the right.

At Tabler Road (within sight of an intersection with Cemetery Road on the left) turn right across the canal, then immediately turn left and follow a footpath with the canal on the left. Soon, at Aux Sable Creek, follow the trail right to Dellos Road. Fellow Dellos Road across the creek. (Notice how the canal is carried over the creek in an aqueduct.) After crossing the creek, veer left to return to the canal. Pass Lock 8 and a small parking lot at the Aux Sable access point.

At an old truss bridge about 100 yards downstream from Lock 8, cross left back over the canal. With the canal on the right, continue west on the former towpath. Eventually, cross a road and continue through the outskirts of Morris. With the canal on the right, continue as the Illinois River comes into view on the left. Cross a road at the entrance to W. G. Stratton State Park.

At the Route 47 bridge, detour left under the bridge, then back up to the path next to the canal. Continue with the canal on the right, then follow the trail across a bridge over the canal and across a road. With the canal on the left, continue west to Gebhard Woods.

12

STARVED ROCK STATE PARK

Walking — 4.5 miles (7.2 kilometers). Rock pinnacles, cliffs and canyons border the Illinois River at Starved Rock State Park. From Starved Rock itself, follow the river upstream past Eagle Cliff to LaSalle Canyon. Return along the rim of the bluffs. Stay back from the edges of the cliffs and control your children closely. Dogs must be leashed. Open daily from dawn until 10:00 P.M. Managed by the Illinois Department of Conservation. Telephone (815) 667-4726.

T HE VIEW FROM STARVED ROCK looks over the Illinois River where it flows through a mile-wide valley that is more than 150 feet lower than the bordering upland. Yet 100,000 years ago, there was neither a valley nor even a river here. Like so many other features in Illinois, the river, cliffs, and tributary canyons at Starved Rock are the product, albeit indirectly, of continental glaciation.

Before the vast glaciers of the Ice Age advanced over the Great Lakes region, central Illinois was part of a large peneplain — that is, a flatland created by prolonged erosion. The peneplain occupied a region of sedimentary rocks formed earlier at the bottom of a shallow sea that covered Illinois — as well as most of the United States, although not all at the same time — in a series of innundations between 500 and 280 million years ago. During each innundation, sand and silt carried to the ocean by rivers settled to the bottom of the sea. Sand, which usually is deposited in river deltas or in water bodies close to shore, was cemented by silica or other minerals

to form sandstone, the main rock type at Starved Rock. Clay and silt, which remain in suspension longer than sand and thus settle to the bottom farther from shore, were compressed and consolidated by the weight of the deposits to form shale. Calcium carbonate, reaching the sea in solution and there precipitated either by organic agencies (such as in skeletons of minute marine animals) or by inorganic processes (such as warming of the water), settled farthest from shore and became limestone. In swamps and other regions of shallow water, plant material accumulated and became beds of coal. Eventually, compressive forces within the earth's crust bowed the rock strata upward and elevated the land above the sea. Erosion followed, then re-submergence. Again and again the cycle of emergence, erosion, and submergence occurred, leading to the formation of various rock strata, some of which are now visible at the surface. Other rock material once overlay what is now visible, but these higher strata were worn away during the period of prolonged erosion that preceded the glacial epoch.

The pre-glacial drainage pattern in Illinois was totally different than the present river system. A major river running from north to south — a predecessor of the Mississippi River — was located about thirty miles to the west of Starved Rock, and a large tributary flowed from east to west about ninety miles to the south. However, during the successive invasions of continental glaciers, the river valleys were filled with clay, sand, and boulders carried and deposited by the ice sheets. Diverted from their channels, the rivers found new courses across the landscape after the glaciers had withdrawn. In places this happened repeatedly with each incursion and recession of the ice. Only after the retreat of the last ice sheet (the Wisconsinan glacier) about 12,500 years ago did the Illinois River assume its present course west from the vicinity of Joliet to Depue, located about fifteen miles west of Starved Rock; at Depue the river joins an older channel and abruptly turns south.

As the last ice sheet retreated during a period that lasted for thousands of years, a series of meltwater torrents, far more

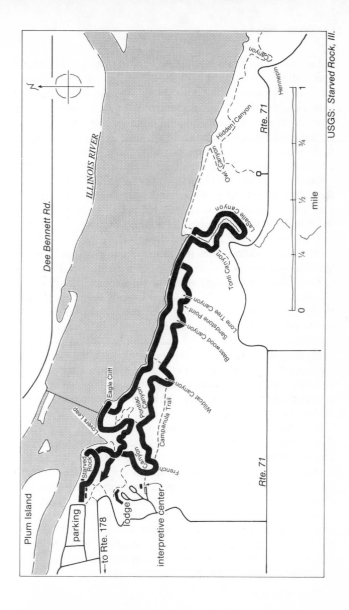

USGS: *Starved Rock, Ill.*

129

voluminous and powerful than the region's present-day rivers, churned through the Illinois Valley. The flow, however, fluctuated in response to various factors. In one often repeated scenario, the clay, sand, and cobbles carried by the glacier were sometimes deposited as long ridges or moraines along the ice front, and the entrapment of meltwater in large lakes behind these moraines produced periods of reduced flow, followed by episodes of rampant erosion when the lakes overflowed and the rivers breached the dike-like moraines. Also, the flow varied as the withdrawal of the ice uncovered other channels that drained part of the meltwater elsewhere. One period of great flow was the Kankakee Torrent, when ice lobes occupying the present-day basins of Lake Michigan, Lake Huron, and Lake Erie cumulatively discharged meltwater from parts of Illinois, Wisconsin, Indiana, and Michigan down the Illinois River. The erosive power of the Kankakee Torrent increased the width of the Illinois Valley by half a mile and lowered the valley floor to the level of what is now the top of Starved Rock, Lovers Leap, and Eagle Cliff. The Kankakee Torrent was followed by a series of floods from glacial Lake Chicago (the precursor of Lake Michigan) after the water broke through the moraine at the Palos Hills, as described in Chapter 7. By the time the Lake Chicago outlet was abandoned for the last time about 2,000 years ago, the river bed at Starved Rock had been lowered 80 to 90 feet to very nearly its present level.

The downward erosion of the main valley in turn led to development of tributary canyons by increasing the gradient — and hence the erosive energy — of small streams where they join the larger river. Following vertical cracks in the bedrock, the tributary streams entrenched themselves in a pattern that reflects the rectilinear jointing characteristic of sandstone formations. (For example, notice how LaSalle Canyon and the stream that carved it make several right-angle turns as they approach the Illinois River.) Erosion was slow while the tributary streams cut into the layer of firmly-cemented, resistant sandstone that now forms the rims of the canyons, but once the streams penetrated to the less firmly cemented material below, erosion was rapid and deep canyons with vertical walls quickly developed. Waterfalls with plunge pools at the bottom have been formed where streams plummet over the upper layer of resistant rock and cut into the relatively soft lower layers. The canyon walls and riverside cliffs also show differential erosion. Weakly cemented layers have receded while the more strongly cemented layers have endured and now stand out, producing a corrugated appearance seen at Starved Rock itself and in the photograph at the beginning of the chapter.

AUTOMOBILE: Starved Rock State Park is located on the Illinois River 120 miles southwest of Chicago. The entrance is on Route 178 about 4 miles south of Interstate 80.

From Chicago — or from the Tri-State Tollway — take Interstate 55 (Stevenson Expressway) south toward St. Louis. West of Joliet, switch to Interstate 80 west toward DeMoine. (If you are coming from Gary or the suburbs south of Chicago, take I-80 west from the outset.) Follow I-80 about 44.7 miles west of the junction with I-55, then take the exit for Route 178 to Utica. Follow Route 178 as it turns left, then right on its way through Utica. Less than half a mile after Route 178 crosses the high bridge over the Illinois River, turn left into Starved Rock State Park. Go 0.6 mile, then turn left, then right into a large parking lot. Park toward the far end — that is, as far east as you can.

WALK: From the eastern end of the parking lot (and with the Illinois River toward the left) head straight 90 yards to the snack bar and other concessions. Turn right through a wide breezeway, then left in front of a flight of stone steps. Follow an asphalt path and (eventually) a flight of wooden stairs up to Starved Rock.

From the boardwalk at the top of Starved Rock, descend on the wooden stairs, then turn left onto a trail marked occasionally with red (and yellow) blazes. (The yellow blazes — which appear on many trails at Starved Rock — indicate merely that you are headed away from the lodge; white blazes indicate that you are headed toward the lodge.)

Follow the red blazes down more stairs. Pass through a skewed four-way intersection, then fork left toward the Canyons, Lovers Leap, and Eagle Cliff. Follow the main, red-blazed trail as it zigzags through the woods and climbs gradually. Eventually, at a T-intersection at the top of the slope, turn left toward Lovers Leap and Eagle Cliff. After 30 yards, fork left and follow the red-blazed trail to Lovers Leap. From Lovers Leap, continue with the river on the left to Eagle Cliff.

From the observation deck at Eagle Cliff, return downriver about 50 yards, then turn left downhill on the red-blazed River Trail. At an intersection, fork left and continue to descend. With the Illinois River on the left, follow the red-blazed trail upstream past mouths of canyons and intersecting trails.

Continue upriver at least as far as LaSalle and Tonti Canyons, just before a large, arched footbridge crosses a cove. Turn right before crossing the bridge. With a stream (or at least a steambed) downhill to the left, follow a green-blazed trail up LaSalle Canyon, across a footbridge, and past a trail intersecting from Tonti Canyon on the right. Eventually, make a U-turn to the left below large cliffs at the head of LaSalle Canyon, then return along the opposite side of the canyon, still with the streambed downhill to the left.

At the mouth of LaSalle Canyon, turn left across the arched footbridge. With the Illinois River on the right, head downstream on the River Trail, maked with red (and white) blazes. At the first intersection, turn left uphill onto the Bluff Trail, marked with brown (and white) blazes.

Climb steeply to the top of the bluff. With the slope

toward the right, follow the Bluff Trail around Lone Tree Canyon, past Sandstone Point, and around the head of Basswood Canyon. At a junction with a trail that intersects from the right, turn left to continue on the Bluff Trail. At the head of Wildcat Canyon, continue along the edge of the cliff past a trail (the Campanula Trail) intersecting from the left. Pass the head of Pontiac Canyon. At a trail intersection, turn left and continue along the rim of the bluff.

Eventually, cross a bridge at the head of French Canyon, then turn right. Continue on the brown-blazed Bluff Trail past a path intersecting from the interpretive center on the left. At the next junction — where the brown (and white) Bluff Trail veers left toward the lodge — fork right onto a trail marked with green (and yellow) blazes. Descend steeply on stairs. At the bottom of the stairs, turn left at a T-intersection. At subsequent intersections, bear left to return to the main parking lot.

13

GREENE VALLEY FOREST PRESERVE

Walking or ski touring — 5 miles (8 kilometers). Passing through meadows, overgrown fields, scrubby woods, and mature forest, the trail links upland and flood plain along the East Branch of the DuPage River. Dogs must be leashed. Open daily from dawn until dusk. Managed by the Forest Preserve District of DuPage County. Telephone (312) 790-4900 or 790-1558.

HOW COME GREENE is this valley? Because a large section of the present-day forest preserve was purchased from the Greene family, whose name in this vicinity goes back more than 150 years. In 1835, only two years after Chicago was incorporated as a village and still eighteen years before railroads linked Chicago to the East Coast, Daniel Moon Greene and his wife acquired 250 acres of rolling prairie, woods, and bottomland along this section of the East Branch of the DuPage River. When the Greene property was surveyed in 1840, the surveyors described the land as "barrens" dotted with scattered and stunted bur, black, and shingle oaks interlaced with wooded ravines and thorny thickets. In 1843 Daniel Green's nephew, William Briggs Greene, bought 200 acres adjoining his uncle's land, and six years later started construction on the first section of a frame house that still stands at the corner of Greene and Hobson Roads. The land remained in the Greene family until it and adjoining tracts, altogether totaling more

than 1,400 acres of former farmland, were acquired by DuPage County to form the Greene Valley Forest Preserve.

A brochure on Greene Valley published by the county speculates that the forest preserve today, with its scattered bur oaks, thickets, scrub, and savannah along the river, may provide a fairly good picture of how the southern part of DuPage County appeared more than a century ago before it become farmland. But one conspicuous feature — the giant Greene Valley Landfill at the southern end of the forest preserve — obviously is new. Constructed of non-hazardous waste, garbage, and fill, this huge mound was started in 1974. Landfill operations are scheduled to continue here until the year 2005, at which time the hill, contoured to the county's specifications, will be converted to recreational use. For the present, however, the landfill operation produces a good deal of noise — particularly an obnoxious and nearly constant *beep-beep-beep* of backing vehicles — so you may want to schedule your visit to the forest preserve on Sunday, when the landfill is closed. Despite its proximity to some of the trails followed by this walk, the landfill is not visually obtrusive. For those who do not yet know this area, Greene Valley is a very pleasant surprise.

AUTOMOBILE: Greene Valley Forest Preserve is located west of Chicago near Woodridge. Access is from Route 53, which runs north and south between Interstate 55 (Stevenson Expressway) and Route 5 (East-West Tollway).

From Chicago take Interstate 290 (Eisenhower Expressway) west, then follow the signs for Route 5 (East-West Tollway) west toward Aurora. Route 5 west can also be reached via the Tri-State Tollway south of O'Hare Airport.

Follow Route 5 west 8.1 miles beyond the first toll plaza, then exit onto Route 53 south. Follow Route 53 south 4.3 miles, then turn right onto 75th Street. Go 0.5 mile, then turn left onto Greene Road. Go another 0.5 mile, then turn right onto 79th Street. After 0.4 mile turn left onto

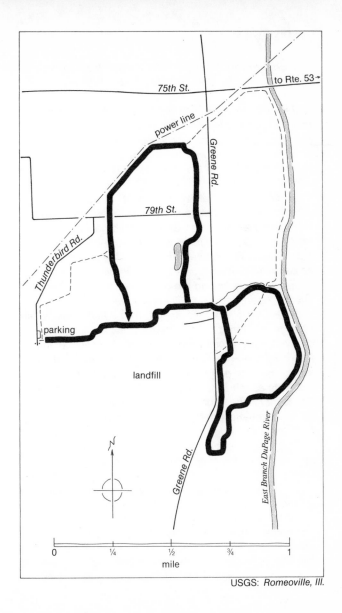

75th St.

to Rte. 53 →

power line

Greene Rd.

79th St.

Thunderbird Rd.

parking

landfill

N

Greene Rd.

East Branch DuPage River

0   ¼   ½   ¾   1

mile

USGS: *Romeoville, Ill.*

137

Thunderbird Road. Follow Thunderbird Road 0.6 mile to the parking lot for Greene Valley Forest Preserve.

WALK: With a weedy field on the left, follow the trail away from the parking lot. At a corner of the field, veer left then right through trees, then continue along the edge of another field dotted with brush and scrub. Pass a trail intersecting from the left. (You will return via this trail at the end of the walk.)

Continue as the trail winds through woods. Eventually, pass another trail intersecting from the left; go straight, then (with caution) cross Greene Road half-right and continue on a trail marked with stakes. About 65 yards from Greene Road, turn right. Follow the trail markers across a field. After crossing a rutted dirt track, bear right in order to skirt around the edge of a large field with Greene Road and a landfill toward the right.

Continue more or less straight as the trail enters an area of large, scattered oaks. Eventually, follow the trail left, then left again around the oak grove. Continue as the trail heads right downhill through a stretch of woods, then along the edge of a field dotted with brush and scrub. Continue as the East Branch of the DuPage River comes into sight on the right. Follow the trail along the flood plain; for the most part, the trail is several dozen yards from the river's edge.

Continue to a trail junction shortly after the path veers left away from the river. At this junction, bear half-right where another trail leads ninety degrees right. With trees and a rivulet on the right and a meadow on the left, follow a grassy path gradually uphill to Greene Road.

Cross the road half-right and follow the trail by which you earlier came in the opposite direction. Pass a meadow and scrubby woods on the right. At the first trail junction, turn right and continue through scrubby woods, then into more mature forest. Pass a pond on the left.

Cross 79th Street and continue across the middle of a meadow toward high electric transmission lines in the distance. At the far end of the field, pass through a hedgerow, then turn left at a T-intersection.

With the transmission lines on the right, follow the trail along the edge of the woods and across a meadow. Turn half-left away from the transmission lines. Cross 79th Street about 50 yards to the left of the intersection with Thunderbird Road. Follow the trail straight through scrubby growth. Continue straight where another trail veers half-right. At a T-intersection, turn right to return to the parking lot.

14

MORTON ARBORETUM

Walking — 2 to 4 miles (3.2 to 6.4 kilometers) depending on which of several trail loops you follow. Actually, you could walk all day here if you wanted to. The arboretum features groves of specimen trees and shrubs, as well as gardens, meadows, and native woods — all interconnected by an extensive trail network. Dogs are prohibited. An admission fee is charged. During the period that daylight saving time is in effect, the arboretum is open daily 9:00 A.M. to dusk (but no later than 7:00 P.M.); during the rest of the year, the arboretum is open 9:00 A.M. to 5:00 P.M. Managed by the Morton Arboretum. Telephone (312) 968-0074.

THE MORTON ARBORETUM, located west of Chicago near Wheaton, comprises more than 1,500 acres of rolling meadows, woods, lakes, and scattered marshes. Joy Morton, one of the early partners in a firm that eventually became the Morton Salt Company under his leadership, started buying land here in 1909 for a country estate, which he called Lisle Farms. Already in 1902 he and his brothers had established a small arboretum at their family home in Nebraska as a memorial to their father, J. Sterling Morton, who was the territorial governor of Nebraska before statehood and later the Secretary of Agriculture under President Cleveland. J. Sterling Morton was also the originator of Arbor Day (now April 22), which grew out of his efforts to encourage Nebraska farmers to plant trees.

In 1921 Joy Morton hired Charles Sargent, director of the

Arnold Arboretum in Boston, to advise him on the development of a major arboretum at Lisle Farms. The aim was to collect from around the world specimens of trees and shrubs that can tolerate the Chicago climate. Sargent thought that Lisle Farms was a suitable site, and accordingly, in 1922 Morton founded the arboretum by placing four hundred acres under the authority of a board of trustees, which he headed until his death in 1934. During the first year of development, Lake Marmo was excavated (all the arboretum lakes are man-made) and 138,000 trees and shrubs were planted. During the following years, Joy Morton and his heirs gave other large tracts to the arboretum, and some adjoining areas were purchased.

The arboretum functions as a research center, school, and park rolled together. One of its chief purposes is to conduct research on tree and scrub culture. Recent projects include the establishment of a program to monitor endangered plant species at the Indiana Dunes National Lakeshore; another ongoing program seeks to develop a hybrid elm tree resistant to the Dutch elm disease. The arboretum also sponsors educational programs ranging from nature walks for school children and adults to courses for college credit. For information about the various lectures, shows, fieldtrips, courses, and other special events offered by the arboretum, call the visitor center.

The Morton Arboretum is the perfect place to learn native and foreign trees or just to walk in a pleasant setting. In the vicinity of the visitor center, the grounds have been attractively landscaped; small signs provide the names of trees and shrubs and other pertinent information. Farther afield, a system of footpaths weaves through woods and meadows. The route shown by the bold line on the map is only one of many possible excursions at the arboretum.

Learning to identify trees is not difficult. Every walk or automobile ride is an opportunity for practice. Notice the overall forms and branching habits of the trees, and also the

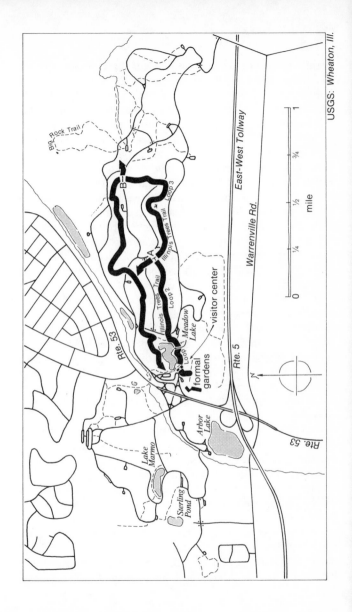

USGS: *Wheaton, Ill.*

143

distinctive qualities of their twigs, buds, bark, leaves, flowers, and fruits or seeds. These factors are the key identification features that distinguish one species from another. Finally, when using a field guide, check the maps or descriptions that delineate the geographic range within which each tree is likely to be found. Near Chicago, however, geographic considerations are problematic because the region lies where the eastern forest (also termed the central hardwood forest), the northern forest, and the Great Plains all adjoin and blend together.

Some trees, of course, have very distinctive and reliable forms. Familiar evergreens like balsam fir and eastern red cedar have a conical shape, like a dunce cap, although in dense stands the red cedar tapers very little and assumes the columnar form of the Italian cypress, which it somewhat resembles. The deciduous little-leaf linden, imported from Europe and used as a street tree, also is more or less conical in shape. The elm displays a spreading form like a head of broccoli. A full-bodied egg-shaped is characteristic of the sugar maple and beech, although both will develop long, branchless trunks in crowded woods, as do most forest trees competing for light. The vertically exaggerated cigar shape of Lombardy poplar — a form called fastigiate — and the pendulous, trailing quality of weeping willow are unmistakable. (Both Lobardy poplar and weeping willow have been introduced to North America from abroad.)

Branching habit, an important clue to some trees, is observable even at a distance. White pine, for example, has markedly horizontal branches with a slight upward tilt at the tips, like a hand turned with its palm up. Norway spruce (another imported species) is usually seen as an ornamental tree dwarfing and darkening a house near which it was planted fifty or a hundred years ago; it is a very tall evergreen with long, evenly spaced, drooping lower branches. The slender lower branches of pin oak slant downward, while those of white oak and red oak often are massive and horizontal, especially on trees growing in the open. The lower branches of the horse chestnut (yet another

European import) also droop but then curl up at the tips in chunky twigs. Elm branches spread up and out like the mouth of a trumpet. The trunk of the mature honeylocust diverges into large branches somewhat in the manner of an elm.

A good botanist or forester can identify trees by their twigs alone — that is, by the end portion of the branch that constitutes the newest growth. During winter the shape, color, size, position, and sheathing of buds are important. For instance, beech buds are long and pointed, tan, and sheathed with overlapping scales like shingles. Sycamore and magnolia buds are wrapped in a single scale. The twigs of horse chestnut are tipped with a big, sticky, brown bud, while those of silver maple, and to a lesser extent of red maple, end with large clusters of red buds. Some oaks, such as white oak, have hairless terminal buds, while other species, such as black oak, have hairy end buds.

Aside from buds, other characteristics of twigs are color, thorns, hair, pith, and the size, shape, and position of leaf scars marking where the leaf stems were attached. For example, most maple twigs are reddish brown, but the twigs of striped maple and mountain maple are greenish. Thorns and spines are significant because relatively few trees have them, notably honeylocust, black locust, Hercules club, prickly ash, buckthorn bumelia, devil's-walkingstick, Osage-orange, American plum, some crab apples, and the many varieties of hawthorn. Most oaks have hairless twigs, although some species such as blackjack oak are distinctly hairy. As for pith, it can be chambered, solid, spongy, or of different colors, depending on the species. Oak and hickory are common forest species near Chicago, but only the pith of white oak in cross section forms a star. Finally, the location of leaf scars in opposite pairs along the twigs (as with maples) distinguishes a wide variety of trees and shrubs from those with leaf scars arranged alternately, first on one side and then on the other (as with oaks). All these distinguishing features can best be appreciated simply by examining the twigs of different species.

Bark is not always a reliable clue for identifying trees, as the color and texture of bark change with age or from trunk to branches to twigs. Often the distinctive character of bark is seen only in the trunks of large, mature trees. Bark can be smooth, furrowed, scaly, plated, shaggy, fibrous, crisscrossed, corky, or papery. Some trees, of course, may be clearly identified by their bark. The names shagbark hickory and paper birch speak for themselves. Striped maple has longitudinal, whitish stripes in the smooth green bark of the younger trees. The crisscrossed ridges of white ash, the light blotches on sycamores, and the smooth gray skin of beech are equally distinctive. Birches and some cherries are characterized by horizontal lenticels like random dashes.

Most people notice leaves, particularly their shape. The leaves of the gray birch are triangular; catalpa, heart-shaped; sweetgum, star-shaped; beech, elliptical (or actually pointed at each end); and black willow narrower still and thus lanceolate. Notice also the leaf margin or edge. Is it smooth like rhododendron, wavy like water oak, serrated like basswood, or deeply lobed like most maples? And how many lobes are there? Tulip-trees, for example, have easily recognized four-lobed leaves; maples have three- or five-lobed leaves. Also, are the lobe tips rounded like white oak or pointed like red oak? Or, maybe, as with sassafras and red mulberry, the same tree has leaves that are shaped differently, the most distinctive being those with a single asymmetical lobe creating a leaf outline like a mitten.

Some leaves such as those of the Japanese maple, horse chestnut, and Ohio buckeye are palmately compound, meaning that they are actually composed of leaflets radiating from the end of the stem like fingers from the palm. In the fall the whole compound leaf drops off the tree as a unit. Other leaves, such as ash, hickory, and sumac, are pinnately compound, being composed of leaflets arranged in opposite pairs along a central stalk. Still other leaves are bipinnately compound, somewhat like a fern. The leaflets grow from stalks that in turn spread from a central stalk. Honeylocust, Kentucky coffeetree, and the ornamental imported silktree are examples.

Although the needles of evergreens are not as varied as the leaves of deciduous plants, there are still several major points to look for, such as the number of needles grouped together. White pine has fascicles of five; pitchpine, loblolly pine, and sometimes shortleaf pine have fascicles of three; and jack pine, red pine, Virginia pine, Austrian pine, and sometimes shortleaf pine have fascicles of two. Needles of spruce, hemlock, and fir grow singly, but are joined to the twig in distinctive ways. Spruce needles grow from little woody pegs, hemlock needles from smaller bumps, and fir needles directly from the twig, leaving a rounded pit when pulled off. Spruce needles tend to be four-sided, hemlock flat, and fir somewhere in between. The needles of larch (also called tamarack) grow in dense clusters and all drop off in winter.

Flowers are a spectacular, though short-lived, feature of some trees and shrubs. Three variables are color, form and (less reliably) time of bloom. Eastern redbud, with red-purple clusters, and shadbush (also called Allegheny serviceberry), with small, white, five-petaled flowers, are among the first of our native trees to bloom. As members of the rose family, apples, cherries, plums, peaches, and hawthorns all have flowers with five petals (usually pink or white) in loose clusters. The blossoms of flowering dogwood consist of four white, petallike bracts, each with a brown notch at the tip, while the flowers of alternate-leaf dogwood consist of loose, white clusters. These are a few of our native species commonly thought of as flowering trees and shrubs, but the blossoms of other native species are equally distinctive, such as the small but numerous flowers of maples or the tuliplike flowers and durable husks of tuliptrees.

Finally, the seeds or fruit of a tree are a conspicuous element in summer and fall, sometimes lasting into winter and even spring. Nobody who sees a tree with acorns could fail to know that it is an oak, although some varieties, such as willow oak and shingle oak (also known as northern laurel oak) are otherwise deceptive. Distinctive nuts are also produced by beech trees, horse chestnut, hickories, and walnut. Some seeds, like ash and maple, have wings. Others, such as honeylocust, Kentucky coffeetree, and redbud, come in pods like beans and in fact are members of the same general legume family. The seeds of birches, poplars, and willows hang in tassels, while those of sweetgum and sycamore form prickle-balls (as do the shells of horse chestnut and buckeye). Eastern cottonwood produces seeds that are windborne by cottonlike tufts. And, of course, brightly colored berries and fruits are produced by many species, such as crabapples, holly, hawthorn, and hackberry. Among needle evergreens, spruce and pine cones hang from the twigs, while fir cones stand upright, and the small hemlock cones grow from the twig tips.

AUTOMOBILE: The Morton Arboretum is located west of Chicago below Wheaton. The entrance is on Route 53 immediately north of the exit off Route 5 (East-West Tollway).

From Chicago take Interstate 290 (Eisenhower Expressway) west, then follow the signs for Route 5 (East-West Tollway) west toward Aurora. Route 5 west can also be reached via the Tri-State Tollway south of O'Hare Airport.

Follow Route 5 west for 8 miles beyond the first toll plaza, then exit onto Route 53 north. Follow Route 53 only 0.2 mile, then turn right into the arboretum east entrance. Follow the curving drive past the visitor center; continue to the visitor center parking lot.

WALK: Start your walk by visiting some of the formal gardens that are unlike most areas at the arboretum. From the courtyard at the visitor center, follow an asphalt path directly away from Meadow Lake. Go only 20 yards, then turn left and follow a brick path to the ground cover

garden, the hedge garden, and the dwarf shrub garden.
After you have seen these attractive formal plantings,
return to the visitor center.

To reach the longer walking trails shown on the map,
descend stone steps leading from the visitor center
courtyard to the edge of Meadow Lake. With the lake on
the left, follow a path (the Illinois Trees Trail, Loop 1) about
one-third of the way around the lake. After passing near a
parking area on the right and treading a short section of
path paved with railroad ties, fork right onto a less worn
trail leading away from the lake and across a road. Follow
a trail (Loop 2 of the Illinois Trees Trail) through woods and
meadow. Loop 2 is blazed with an occasional red-painted
impression of an oak leaf on top of a concrete post.

At a T-intersection (marked A on the map), turn left to
circle 0.8 more miles back to the visitor center, or turn
right to continue on a longer loop (Loop 3, green blazes)
that circles 2 more miles back to the visitor center.

At a point where Loop 3 crosses a road (marked B on
the map), it is possible to add yet another 1.2 miles to
your walk. To do so, follow the road right from point B. Go
a few dozen yards to an intersection, then bear left across
the grass to another road in the distance. Follow this road
to the right and into the woods. Where a footpath crosses
the road, turn left on the Big Rock Trail circuit. When you
again reach the road, return to Loop 3 and continue on
the circuit back to the visitor center.

15

ILLINOIS PRAIRIE PATH
Wheaton to Elgin

Walking, bicycling, or ski touring — up to 14 miles (22.5 kilometers) one way. Walk from Wheaton to the outskirts of Elgin (or vice versa) along an old railroad that now forms a hiker's highway through woods, fields, and marsh. The ties and rails have been removed and the trail paved with hard-packed limestone grit. If you do not want to retrace your steps, a car shuttle is necessary. For a shorter excursion, start or stop at one of the road crossings shown on the map. Managed by The Illinois Prairie Path, P.O. Box 1086, Wheaton, Illinois 60189.

THE ILLINOIS PRAIRIE PATH extends from Wheaton in three directions, like a Y turned on its side toward the left, thus: ➤. Wheaton is located at the center where the two arms and the leg converge. One arm stretches northwest fourteen miles to Elgin, the other arm goes southwest twelve miles to Aurora, and the leg extends east fifteen miles through Elmhurst to the Des Plaines River, although in each case the trail deteriorates in quality toward the end. Only the section between Wheaton and Elgin is described here; it provides a good day's outing by itself and an introduction to the Wheaton trailhead, where the Aurora and Elmhurst sections also begin.

The Illinois Prairie Path follows the former roadbed of the Chicago Aurora and Elgin Railroad, an electric commuter line

which suspended passenger service in 1957, after operating for more than half a century. During its life the line not only served the cities mentioned in its name, but also contributed to the rapid suburbanization of the region west of Chicago.

The railroad corporation was chartered in 1899, but construction did not begin until 1901. The Aurora branch opened in 1902, and nine months later the line from Wheaton to Elgin was completed, as well as a spur off the Aurora branch to Batavia. (This spur is also part of The Prairie Path.) At first the eastern terminus was at Laramie Avenue just inside the Chicago boundary, but starting in 1905 the trains continued intown all the way to the Loop on the Metropolitan West Side Elevated. In 1909 yet another western spur was added, branching off the Elgin line a little northwest of Wheaton and running to Geneva and St. Charles on the Fox River. (This spur may eventually be added to The Prairie Path.) The headquarters, yard, and repair shops were in Wheaton at the junction of the Aurora and Elgin branches. Although the railroad operated as a trolley through the city streets of Aurora and some other towns, along most of the right-of-way the trains drew current from a 600-volt third rail, earning for the line the nickname of the Great Third Rail.

In its early years the Great Third Rail prospered. Its electric coaches were fast and also cleaner and cheaper to ride than the sooty, coal-fired trains of the competing steam railroads. By 1914 the company had seventy wooden coaches and even two parlor-buffet cars named Carolyn and Florence, where for an extra twenty-five cents — which also could be applied toward an order of food — passengers sat in individual plush leather chairs.

Following World War I, however, the Great Third Rail began to lose money. The physical plant had deteriorated, and because of inflation during the post-war years, costs exceeded revenues. Creditors successfully petitioned to have the railroad placed in receivership. In 1922 the company was reorganized and equipped with new steel passenger coaches. Using electric

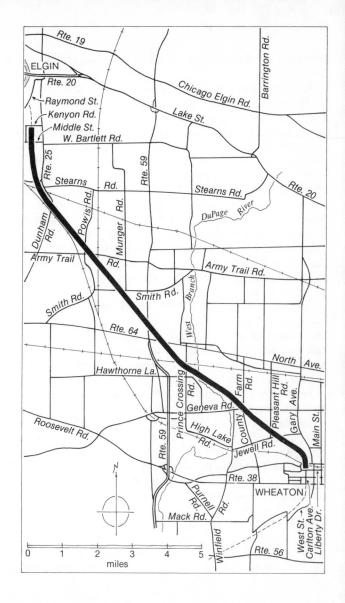

locomotives, the revivified CA&E also inaugurated freight service.

In 1926 Samuel Insull's Middle West Utilities purchased control of the railroad. Insull already had gained control of Chicago's transit system (which like the CA&E was a privately-run, for-profit affair), and after numerous mergers he had expanded his operations throughout Illinois and into neighboring states. In 1912 he had formed a complex of companies with interlocking directorates that operated over three hundred steam plants, almost two hundred hydroelectric generating plants, and numerous other power plants throughout the United States. For a few years the CA&E prospered under Insull's regime, but in 1932 his electric utilities empire collapsed. The Great Third Rail again failed and was placed in receivership that lasted throughout the Depression and World War II.

Riders increased during the war, largely because gasoline rationing curtailed automobile travel. The company's freight business also prospered. In 1946 the line finally emerged from its protracted receivership as suburban development boomed and rush-hour commuter traffic increased. Weekend traffic, however, declined abruptly as people turned to cars for leisuretime excursions and as the five-day work week eliminated the commuter rush on Saturday.

In 1952 the CA&E management petitioned the Illinois Commerce Commission to be allowed to replace its trains with buses because the elevated tracks west from Chicago were scheduled to be torn down to make room for the Congress Street Expressway. Although the Illinois Commerce Commission refused to allow the CA&E to discontinue its commuter rail service altogether, it authorized the company to terminate its trains at Forest Park. There passengers could transfer to the trains of the Chicago Transit Authority, by now a public agency. Operating on temporary, ground-level tracks during the period of highway construction, the Chicago transit trains were forced to stop at every grade crossing on their way toward the Loop. Within a week after the new system went into effect, thousands of Third Rail riders switched to automobiles or to the competing Chicago and North Western Railroad. Soon the Great Third Rail was losing nearly $1 million per year. In mid-1957 the company successfully petitioned to suspend passenger service temporarily, and at 12:10 P.M. on July 3, the commuter trains stopped running and returned (for the last time, as matters developed) to the Wheaton yard. Chicago's afternoon newspapers carried banner headlines advising CA&E passengers to find other transportation home.

For the next three years a series of commuter committees were organized to seek ways to resuscitate passenger service. Freight operations continued for two years, then ceased. In 1960 a proposal to form a governmental agency to purchase and operate the defunct line was rejected by voters after vigorous opposition from the Chicago and North Western Railroad and a local bus company. Finally, the CA&E applied for permission to abandon the line, and the request was approved effective July 10, 1961.

The transformation of the abandoned roadbed into a public path is yet another story. The idea originated with Mrs. May Theilgaard Watts, a naturalist at the Morton Arboretum and author of *Reading the Landscape of America,* a collection of popular essays on plant ecology. A small corps of backers generated public support for the railroad path by giving hundreds of illustrated talks and leading dozens of fieldtrips. They also sought and received the necessary cooperation of utility companies and of state, county, and local officials. In 1965 the group formed The Illinois Prairie Path, a non-profit corporation which the following year leased the railroad right-of-way in DuPage County from the county government, its new owner. In 1972 the Illinois Department of Conservation acquired the Kane County segments of the right-of-way and then leased the property to be County Forest Preserve District for use as part of The Prairie Path. And in 1979 the state acquired 4.5 miles of right-of-way in Cook County to be managed by the trail corporation.

The Illinois Prairie Path is administered by an unpaid board of directors elected annually by the membership. There are no paid Prairie Path employees. The many improvements that have been made along the trail, including surfacing the path with limestone grit and the construction of new bridges, have been paid for by members' dues and by donations. Much work was done by volunteers, as continues to be the case. If you would like to join The Prairie Path or simply want more information, send a letter enclosing a self-addressed stamped envelop to The Illinois Prairie Path, P.O. Box 1086, Wheaton, Illinois 60189.

AUTOMOBILE: The Prairie Path starts in Wheaton west of Chicago. The trailhead is at the end of Carlton Avenue 0.3 mile north of the intersection with Route 38 (Roosevelt Road).

From Chicago take Interstate 290 (Eisenhower Expressway) west, then follow the signs for Route 5 (East-West Tollway) west toward Aurora. Route 5 west can also be reached via the Tri-State Tollway south of O'Hare Airport.

Follow Route 5 west for 8 miles beyond the first toll plaza, then exit onto Route 53 north. Follow Route 53 for 4 miles. Just before the underpass at Route 38 (Roosevelt Road), turn left onto the ramp leading up to Route 38. Turn left onto Route 38 itself and follow it west for more than 3 miles through Wheaton. Of course, Wheaton can also be reached by following Route 38 (Roosevelt Road) west all the way from Chicago.

As you head west through Wheaton on Route 38, pass the Wheaton Central Community High School on the right, then an intersection with Main Street on the right. Continue 0.5 mile beyond Main Street, then turn right onto Carlton Avenue. Go 0.3 mile to a T-intersection with Liberty Drive. The intersection of Carlton Avenue and Liberty Drive is the zero-mile point on The Prairie Path.

If, after walking on The Prairie Path, you do not want to

retrace your steps to Wheaton Center, a car shuttle is necessary. Obviously, a shuttle involves either two cars and two driver-hikers, or a driver who simply meets you at the other end. As the map shows, the path crosses roads periodically. You can use the map to shuttle a car to the road-crossing where you want to end your trip. Dunham Road at 10.7 miles is a good stopping point, and so is Kenyon Road at 13 miles.

WALK: From the intersection of Carlton Avenue and Liberty Drive in Wheaton, follow The Prairie Path uphill and across a bridge. After about 0.5 mile, pass Lincoln Marsh on the left. At about 1.5 miles, cross Jewell Road, then Pleasant Hill Road. At 2.5 miles, cross the intersection of Geneva Road and County Farm Road, where there is a small parking lot immediately west of the crossroads. Continue straight through the woods to a small bridge over the West Branch of the DuPage River at 4.3 miles. This is a good place to stop and turn around if you are walking and must return to Wheaton.

The Prairie Path continues northwest across Prince Crossing Road at 4.7 miles, where there is an old power substation for the railway. Continue through the woods and across a railroad. At about 5.5 miles, pass under Route 64. Cross Route 59 (near an intersection with Oak Road) at 6.6 miles, then cross Smith Road (near an intersection with Munger Road) at 7.4 miles. Cross a railroad at 8.6 miles, then Army Trail Road at 8.9 miles, and soon afterwards, Powis Road. Continue through fields, marsh, and swamp on a very attractive section of The Prairie Path, reaching Dunham Road at 10.7 miles.

Northwest of Dunham road, the quality of the path surface deteriorates, but the trail still is adequate for walking or for rugged bicycles. To continue, cross Dunham Road obliquely. Follow the path across a railroad at 11.2 miles and Route 25 soon afterward. Continue

157

uphill. Cross Middle Street at 12.5 miles and Kenyon Road, site of the Clintonville Station, at 13 miles. This is a good stopping place, although the trail is passable for another mile to Raymond Street in South Elgin.

16

CRABTREE NATURE CENTER

*Walking — 3 miles (4.8 kilometers). The chief attraction here
is variety: farm fields, orchard, meadow, woods, prairie,
marshes, and ponds. Dogs are prohibited. Open daily
(except Thanksgiving, Christmas, and New Year's Day) 8:00
A.M. to a half-hour before sunset. Managed by the Forest
Preserve District of Cook County. Telephone (312) 261-8400
from the city or 366-9420 from the suburbs.*

THERE IS VERY LITTLE PRAIRIE LEFT in the Prairie
State. To see the grassland that once typified much of northern
Illinois, you have to visit one of the various parks where big
bluestem grass, blazing star, prairie dock, and other native
plants have been re-established in an attempt to show what the
region may have looked like before the prairie was plowed and
planted into oblivion.

Near Chicago a number of prairie restoration projects are
underway. Although not the largest, the prairie at Crabtree
Nature Center is one of the most attractive because the clumps
of trees that occupy the hollows and stream banks block views
of any extraneous development that might otherwise mar the
prairie atmosphere. Here is a chance to walk through a landscape that in part resembles what the first settlers saw nearly
everywhere in northern Illinois when they arrived 150 years
ago.

The tall-grass prairie formerly covered an immense triangular area at the middle of the continent; one corner was in
northwestern Indiana, another corner in southern Manitoba,

and the third corner in Oklahoma. To the west the tall grasses gave way to the sparser, shorter grasses of the Great Plains. Within the prairie area, most forests were limited to major stream valleys, although scattered groves of oak and hickory sometimes occurred on knolls, where the soil had a lower peat content and was not as soggy or as acidic as the poorly-drained flatland and hollows. Also, thickets of hawthorn, crabapples, quaking aspen, and burr oak sometimes encroached on the grassland. Published in 1868, the *Geological Survey of Illinois* states: "The proportion of prairie to wooded land [in Cook County] is a little greater than two to one. The timber is distributed in belts, of varying width, along the water-courses and on the shore of the lake, with frequent groves or timber islands in the open prairie." In DeKalb, Kane, and DuPage Counties to the west, the proportion of prairie to forest was estimated at three or four to one.

How the grassland originated and remained largely treeless for thousands of years has been the subject of much research and debate. Although ample rain falls on the eastern prairie (about thirty-three inches annually in Illinois), a warm, dry period that followed the retreat of the last glacier may initially have fostered the spread of grasses because they tolerate drought better than trees.

Once the prairie was established, a variety of factors, of which fire is the chief, enabled the grassland to hold its own against woody invasion. Started by lightning or by Indians, fires swept over any given expanse of prairie every few years, feeding on the annual accumulation of dry, dead leaves. These fires killed the seedlings of most woody plants but not the grasses themselves. Growing from underground stems (or rhisomes) and drawing nourishment from roots that pentrate six feet or more below the surface, the grasses quickly sprouted back after each blaze. In fact, studies show that as much as ninety percent of each plant's mass may be underground, where it is simply unaffected by fire. A fire in spring even appears to hasten the growth of prairie vegetation. In order to attract

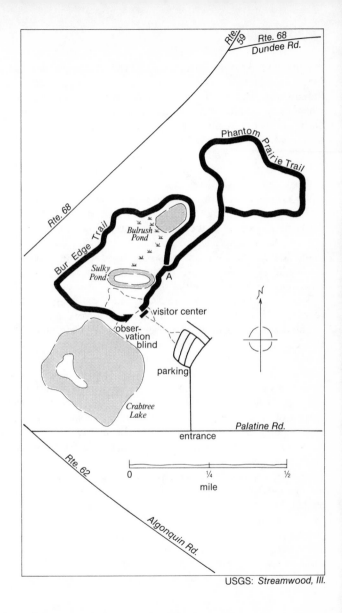

Rte. 59
Rte. 68
Dundee Rd.

Phantom Prairie Trail

Rte. 68

Bur Edge Trail

Bulrush
Pond

Sulky
Pond

A

visitor center

obser-
vation
blind

parking

Crabtree
Lake

Palatine Rd.

entrance

0   ¼   ½
mile

Rte. 62

Algonquin Rd.

USGS: *Streamwood, Ill.*

163

grazing animals to the fresh grass that sprouts after each blaze, Indians are thought to have set fires as a regular practice. The Indians also used fire to drive bison and pronghorn to places where they could be killed by hunters or stampeded over bluffs. In recognition of the importance of fire in prairie ecology, carefully controlled fires are set each spring in the grassland at the Crabtree Nature Center.

In addition to fire, other factors helped to maintain the prairie free of trees. Bison and pronghorn hindered the growth of woody plants by trampling and grazing on the seedlings and rubbing and scratching themselves against young trees. The dense root systems of the prairie plants made it difficult for seeds of trees to sprout and grow. The grasses exhausted the available water near the surface so that there was none left over for seedlings. Also, before ditches were dug to drain large areas for agriculture, much of the prairie — particulary in flat regions — was unsuited for trees because it was soggy or even covered with water for two or three months every spring.

The dominant plant of the tall-grass prairie is big bluestem, also called turkey foot grass because its three-pronged seed head resembles a bird's foot. It is an excellent forage crop and often was used by the settlers to feed livestock. Found in rich, moderately drained soils, big bluestem produces a seed stalk as much as six or eight feet tall. Despite its annual seed head, this grass propagates itself mainly by rhisomes that spread outward underground to establish new plants. In this way, large areas are quickly occupied and tenaciously held against competing plants.

Indian grass is another widespread native prairie plant, similar in appearance to big bluestem except in mid-August, when reddish-brown tassels form at the ends of the seed stalks. Switch grass, which has a slight bend in the stem at the joints or nodes, is also common. Indian grass and switch grass both thrive in disturbed areas, but Indian grass favors somewhat dry soil and switch grass prefers moist soil.

In low, undrained areas, other tall grasses take over —

predominantly cordgrass and blue-joint grass, both of which can tolerate prolonged flooding during spring and early summer and long dry spells during the late summer and fall. Cordgrass is the tallest prairie grass; its seed stalks commonly reach eight to twelve feet. Its finely serrated leaf edges are very sharp and can cut like a knife. In July flowers that resemble combs appear along the top foot of the stalks. Blue-joint grass, which has coarse, bluish-green leaves, forms white seed heads when it blooms early in July.

In areas of dry, sandy soil, shorter grasses predominate. Here, little bluestem and side-oats grama are most abundant, growing to knee height when mature. Little bluestem is common in the western prairie; its root system penetrates to a depth of twenty feet and enables it to survive severe drought. On the driest sites, muhley grass and blue and hairy grama are likely to be found, growing not more than a few inches high. All of these dry grasses are bunch grasses; they grow in tight bunches which increase in diameter only slightly each year. The plants occupy only a small portion of the ground surface, leaving bare soil between, but the roots and leaves reach out into the intervening spaces, preventing other plants from growing there.

Aside from various grasses, the prairie vegetation is also characterized by numerous forbs — a catch-all term meaning any herbaceous plant other than grasses. Many are members of the daisy and pea families and have colorful flowers that dominate the prairie scene before the tall grasses bloom. Like the grasses, the forbs are perennials, growing afresh each year from roots that may live for decades and that enable them to survive episodic fires and droughts.

AUTOMOBILE: The Crabtree Nature Center is located northwest of Chicago near Barrington Hills. The entrance is on Palatine Road 0.5 mile east of the intersection with Route 62 (Algonquin Road).

From Chicago take Interstate 90 (Kennedy Expressway) northwest toward O'Hare Airport and Rockford. As you

approach O'Hare, stay on I-90 as it becomes the Northwest Tollway toward Rockford and Elgin. The Northwest Tollway can also be reached via the Tri-State Tollway east of O'Hare Airport.

Follow I-90 (the Northwest Tollway) about 8.4 miles beyond the first toll plaza, then take the exit for Route 53 north toward Rolling Meadows. Follow Route 53 about 4 miles to the exit for Palatine Road west. From the bottom of the exit ramp, follow Palatine Road west 8.1 miles to the entrance to Crabtree Nature Center on the right.

The Crabtree Nature Center can also be reached by following Willow Road west from the vicinity of Winetka or Northfield. West of Milwaukee Avenue, Willow Road becomes Palatine Road. As noted in the preceding paragraph, the nature center is located about 8 miles west of Route 53.

WALK: The trails start at a terrace behind the visitor center building. (The terrace is reached by passing through the visitor center or by following a path that forks right about 80 yards in front of the visitor center.) With your back to the visitor center, turn right and follow a path paved at first with asphalt, then with wood chips. Fork right for the Bur Edge Trail and continue past Sulky Pond. At a fork in the trail (marked A on the map), bear right for the Phantom Prairie Trail circuit, about 1.7 miles in length.

After completing the Phantom Prairie loop, return to the trail junction at point A on the map, then turn right to continue counter-clockwise around the Bur Edge Trail circuit (1.3 miles) and back to the visitor center.

17

LAKEWOOD FOREST PRESERVE

Walking or ski touring — 1 or more miles (1.6 or more kilometers). A network of trails explores a rolling landscape of forest, fields, ponds, and marsh. Dogs must be leashed. Open daily 8:00 A.M. until sunset. Managed by the Lake County Forest Preserve District. Telephone (312) 367-6640.

Y OU MAY HAVE HEARD of cruises to nowhere: a voyage without destination or ports of call, purely for the pleasure of being out on the open ocean. Here is the sylvan equivalent: a woodland walk to nowhere. This excursion follows bridle paths through forest and former farmland, without particular highlights along the way, but thoroughly pleasant nonetheless.

Bird identification is the subject of Chapter 6; a related rainy-day pastime is bird names. After all, as a word, *titmouse,* for example, is worth a smile by itself, and although a titmouse is easy to identify, how many birders know what *titmouse* means? Why is a petrel so called? And what about *killdeer, turnstone, nuthatch,* and other curious bird names?

Although many American Indian place names (Chicago, for example) were adopted by the Europeans, the settlers and early ornithologists made a clean sweep when it came to naming — or rather, renaming — North American birds. In a few cases where the same species (brant, for instance) were found on both sides of the Atlantic, use of the European name was a matter of course. More generally, however, the settlers simply

re-used the names of Old World birds for similar-looking —
but actually different — New World species. The English, for
example, have given the name *robin* to various red-breasted
birds in India, Australia, and North America. More often still,
the use of general names like *wren* was extended to American
birds, with the addition of qualifying words to identify individual species (house wren, Carolina wren, and so forth).
However, scientific classification has sometimes placed whole
categories of American birds in entirely different families than
their European namesakes, as in the case of American warblers; the only North American birds in the same family as the
European warblers are the gnatcatcher and kinglets — not at all
what are called warblers here. Finally, in relatively rare instances, American birds have been given unique and frequently
colorful new names based on their appearance, song, and
behavior, as, for instance, the canvasback, whip-poor-will, and
yellow-bellied sapsucker.

Early ornithologists seem to have been quite casual about
naming birds. Alexander Wilson (1766-1813), who is generally regarded as the father of American ornithology, once shot a
bird in a magnolia tree; hence, *magnolia warbler* for a bird
whose preferred habitat is low, moist conifers. Usually, however, Wilson named birds by the locality where his specimens
were collected, as with the Nashville warbler and the Savannah
(Georgia) sparrow. Not surprisingly, many of the geographic
names given to birds by early ornithologists bear no relation to
the species' breeding territory or winter range; the Savannah
sparrow, for example, is found throughout North America and
might just as well have been named for Chicago or even
Anchorage. Among the Tennessee, Connecticut, and Kentucky
warblers (all named by Wilson), only the last is at all likely to
be found in its nominal state during the breeding season, and
none winter north of Mexico. But probably the greatest geographic misnomer among bird names is our native turkey, after
the supposed region of its origin. The name was first applied to
the guinea cock, which was imported from Africa through

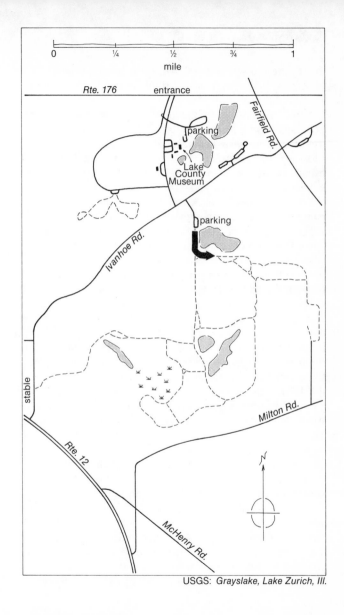

0   ¼   ½   ¾   1
mile

Rte. 176   entrance

parking

Lake
County
Museum

Fairfield Rd.

parking

Ivanhoe Rd.

stable

Milton Rd.

Rte. 12

N

McHenry Rd.

USGS: *Grayslake, Lake Zurich, Ill.*

Turkey into Europe and with which the American bird was for a time identified when it was first introduced to Europe in about 1530.

Some bird names, although seeming to refer to specific geographic areas, are actually far broader in their historical meaning. *Louisiana* in Louisiana heron refers to the vast territory of the Louisiana Purchase, even though the bird is usually found only in coastal areas. This species was first collected on the Lewis and Clark Expedition and was named by Wilson. *Arcadia,* as in Arcadian flycatcher, is an old French name for Nova Scotia, but the term was used generally to suggest a northern clime, as was also *boreal* in boreal chickadee, from the Greek god of the north wind, Boreas.

In addition to birds named *by* early ornithologists and explorers, there are birds named *for* them. Wilson, for example, is memorialized in the name of a petrel, a phalarope, a plover, a warbler, and also a genus of warblers. John James Audubon is honored by Audubon's shearwater and "Audubon's" warbler, a form of the yellow-rumped warbler. There was a measure of reciprocity about this last bird name: in 1837 John Kirk Townsend, a Philadelphia ornithologist and bird collector, named "Audubon's" warbler, and a year or two later Audubon returned the favor with Townsend's solitaire. Then there are species named for ornithologists' wives, daughters, and relatives, as in Anna's hummingbird and Virginia's, Lucy's, and Grace's warblers. Some birds bear human names connected to no one in particular. Guillemot (French for "little William"), magpie (in part based on Margaret), martin ("little Mars"), and parakeet ("little Peter") are all thought to be pet names or affectionate tags that have become attached to various species.

Color is probably the dominant theme in bird names. Plumages cover the spectrum, ranging from the red phalarope through the orange-crowned warbler, yellow rail, green-winged teal, blue goose, indigo bunting, purple gallinule, and violet-crowned hummingbird. For stripped-down straightforwardness there are names like bluebird and blackbird. For grandiloquence (or is it precision?) there is the cerulean warbler. For meaninglessness there is the clay-colored sparrow. (What color is that?) Some bird names less obviously denote basic hues: vireo (green), oriole (golden), dunlin ("little dull-brown one"), canvasback (for its speckled gray and white back), brant (thought by some to mean "burnt," referring to the dusky black plumage), and waxwing (whose red-tipped secondary wing feathers recalled to someone the color and substance of sealing wax).

Shape or other distinctive features often are reflected in bird names. The profile of the bufflehead suggests an American buffalo. The loggerhead shrike has a disproportionately large head. Shovelers have long, broad bills. The word *falcon* is derived from a Latin term for "sickle," suggesting the bird's curved talons. From head to toe, there is a body part that is some bird's nominal identity: tufted titmouse, horned lark, eared grebe (*grebe* itself may come from a Breton word for "crest"), ruffed grouse, pectoral sandpiper (for the air sack under its breast feathers), stilt sandpiper (for its comparatively long legs), rough-legged hawk (for its feathered tarsi), sharp-shinned hawk (it has), semi-palmated sandpiper (for its partially webbed feet), and Lapland longspur (for the elongated claw on the hind toe).

Some names indicate size, from *great* and *greater* to *little, lesser,* and *least.* Symmetry would seem to demand a *greatest,* but perhaps that need is filled by *king,* which occasionally refers to stature. The king rail, for example, is the largest of the rails. But sometimes *king* is simply a compliment to a bird's raiment or a reference to distinguishing plumage on its crown, as in the ruby-crowned and golden-crowned kinglets ("little kings"). *Gallinule* itself suggests size, being derived from Latin for "little hen." *Starling* is from the Anglo-Saxon word for bird; with the addition of the diminutive suffix *-ling,* it simply means "little bird." *Titmouse* similarly is a combination of Icelandic and Anglo-Saxon meaning "small bird." Thus one of our most curious names has a prosaic explanation.

A few names, like that of the gull-billed tern, make explicit comparisons with other birds. The lark bunting sings on the wing like a skylark, the curlew sandpiper has a downwardly curved, curlew-like bill. The swallow-tailed kite has a deeply forked tail like a barn swallow. The turkey vulture has a head that somewhat resembles that of a turkey. And *cormorant* is derived from French for "sea crow."

Many bird names refer to distinctive behavior. Woodpeckers, sapsuckers, creepers, and wagtails all do what their names suggest. Turnstones do indeed turn over small stones and shells while searching for food. *Black skimmer* describes the bird's technique of sticking its lower bill into the water while flying just above the surface. *Shearwater* similarly suggests the bird's skimming flight. Frigatebirds were named by sailors for the birds' piratical habit of pursuing and robbing other birds. *Duck* is derived from Anglo-Saxon for "diver." *Nuthatch* is from "nut hack," referring to the bird's technique of wedging a nut into a crevice and then hacking it into small pieces. *Vulture* is akin to Latin *vellere*, "to pluck or tear." Although many people associate *loon* with the bird's lunatic laugh, as in "crazy as a loon," more likely the word is derived from a Norse term for "lame," describing the bird's awkwardness on land — a result of its legs being very near its tail. There is, however, at least one North American bird that is named for its mental capacity: the booby. Seamen who raided the isolated colonies thought the birds stupid because they were unaccustomed to predators and inept at protecting themselves. The dotterel (whose name is related to "dolt" and "dotage") is another nominally foolish bird. Ernest A. Choate, in his fascinating *Dictionary of American Bird Names,* and Edward S. Gruson, in *Words for Birds,* discuss these and other names.

Some birds, such as the whistling swan, whooping crane, clapper rail, piping plover, laughing gull, mourning dove, warbling vireo, and chipping sparrow, are named for how they sound. *Oldsquaw* suggests this duck's noisy, garrulous voice. The catbird mews and the grasshopper sparrow trills and

buzzes like the insect. Gruson, however, says that the grasshopper sparrow is named for its diet, as are the goshawk (literally, "goosehawk") and oystercatchers, flycatchers, and gnatcatchers. The saw-whet owl is named for the bird's endlessly repeated note, which is supposed to suggest the sound of a saw being sharpened with a whetstone. The bittern, whose name ultimately is traceable to its call, has a colorful assortment of descriptive folk names, including "bog-bumper," "stake driver," "thunder pumper," and "water belcher." The song sparrow and mute swan are named simply for the fact that they are comparatively vocal or silent. The evening grosbeak and vesper sparrow both tend to sing at dusk. Finally, of course, many birds' songs or calls are also their names, including the bobolink, bobwhite, bulbul, chachalaca, chickadee, chuckwill's-widow, crow, cuckoo, curlew, dickcissel, killdeer, kittiwake, owl, pewee, phoebe, towhee, veery, whimbrel, whippoor-will, and willet. *Quail* (like "quack") and *raven* are thought originally to have been imitative of bird calls.

Habitat is a major theme of bird names, as with the surf scoter, sandpiper, sanderling ("little one of the sand"), seaside sparrow, marsh hawk, waterthrush, meadowlark, wood duck, bushtit, and field, swamp, and tree sparrows. Then there is the *kind* of tree or shrub, as in spruce and sage grouse, cedar waxwing, myrtle warbler, pine siskin, and orchard oriole. The tree, bank, cliff, and barn swallows are named for their preferred nesting sites. As for *prairie warbler,* the name is simply a misnomer; the bird is common east of the Mississippi and usually is found in brushy, scrubby areas.

Several bird names are associated with human figures. Petrels are thought to be named for Saint Peter, who walked on the water at Lake Genneserath; when landing in the water, petrels dangle their feet and hesitate for a moment, thus appearing to stand on the waves. Cardinals, of course, are named for the red robes and hats of the churchmen. The bizarre and contrasting pattern of the harlequin duck suggests the traditional costume of Italian pantomime.

Finally, there is the ovenbird, almost unique among North American birds for being named after the appearance of its nest, which is built on the forest floor and resembles a miniature Dutch oven. "Basketbird" and "hangnest" are folk names referring to the pendulous nests of orioles.

AUTOMOBILE: Lakewood Forest Preserve is located northwest of Chicago near Wauconda. The main entrance is on Route 176 about 2.4 miles east of Route 12.

From Chicago take Interstate 90 (Kennedy Expressway) northwest toward O'Hare Airport and Rockford. As you approach O'Hare, stay on I-90 as it becomes the Northwest Tollway toward Rockford and Elgin. The Northwest Tollway can also be reached via the Tri-State Tollway east of O'Hare Airport.

Follow I-90 (the Northwest tollway) about 8.4 miles beyond the first toll plaza, then take the exit for Route 53 north toward Rolling Meadows. Follow Route 53 about 6 miles to the exit for Route 68 (Dundee Road). (Presently, there is only one exit ramp at Route 68, but if a full cloverleaf is ever built, take the westbound exit.) At the top of the exit ramp, turn left (or, if a westbound exit has been built, merge smoothly onto Route 68). Go 1 mile west on Route 68, then turn right onto Route 12 (Rand Road). This intersection can also be reached by following Route 68 west from the vicinity of Glencoe or east from Carpentersville.

From the intersection of Route 68 (Dundee Road) and Route 12 (Rand Road), follow Route 12 northwest 11.4 miles to the exit for Route 176 (Liberty Road). From the bottom of the exit ramp, turn right and follow Route 176 for 2.4 miles through Wauconda to the entrance to Lakewood Forest Preserve on the right.

Follow the asphalt entrance drive only 0.1 mile; where a gravel road continues straight, bear left to a four-way intersection, and there turn right. Go 0.3 mile to a T-

intersection with Ivanhoe Road. Turn left and go about 100 yards, then turn right at the first opportunity onto a gravel road marked with symbols for fishing, riding, hiking, and parking. Follow the gravel road 0.1 mile to the parking lot.

Finally, yet another approach to Lakewood Forest Preserve is via Route 176 from the east. Route 176 originates in Lake Bluff and crosses Route 41 (Skokie Road), Route 43 (Waukegan Road), Interstate 94 (Tri-State Tollway), Route 21 (Milwaukee Road), and passes through Libertyville and Mundelein on its way to Wauconda. The forest preserve entrance is the first left-hand turn after Fairfield Road.

WALK: From the back of the parking lot, follow a gravel road past a pond on the left. Fork left at the first opportunity just beyond the pond, and from there use the map to navigate a route of your own choosing through the trail network.

When you are done with your walk, you may want to visit the Lake County Museum, for which the parking lot is just north of the museum (see the map).

18

MORAINE HILLS STATE PARK

Walking, bicycling, or ski touring — 3.5 or 7 miles (5.6 or 11.3 kilometers), depending on whether you take one loop or two, as outlined on the map. And for a still longer excursion, you can circle Lake Defiance. The trails meander through an intriguing landscape of knolls, ridges, marshes, and lakes, seemingly distributed without rhyme or reason. Dogs must be leashed. Open daily (except Christmas) for hours that correspond approximately with daylight. Managed by the Illinois Department of Conservation. Telephone (815) 385-1624.

A NUMBER OF PARKS near Chicago could aptly be named "Moraine Hills." In addition to the actual Moraine Hills State Park that is explored in this chapter, there are the Palos Hills, Waterfall Glen, Crabtree Nature Center, Lakewood Forest Preserve, Volo Bog, and, of course, the Kettle Moraine in southern Wisconsin — all of which show the telltale juxtaposition of hummocks and hollows characteristic of moraines.

But what, exactly, is a moraine, and how is one formed? The following is a brief discussion of glacial processes that account for the appearance of much of the landscape near Chicago.

Glaciers are simply the result of the accumulation of snow over a period of many years, as frequently occurs at higher elevations and higher latitudes, where the total annual fall of snow exceeds what annually melts or evaporates. As the snow thaws during the day and refreezes at night, it packs down and becomes granular and then turns to ice. When the ice has

accumulated to a thickness of about one hundred feet, it becomes plastic under its own weight and is able to flow, in some instances more than a hundred feet per day. The surface, however, remains brittle so that large cracks or *crevasses* develop as the plastic ice below moves under the force of gravity.

Photographs of Alaska, the Alps, and other mountainous regions have made familiar to everyone the image of glaciers flowing like rivers of ice down mountainsides and along broad valleys. As big as they are, these glaciers are small compared to *continental glaciers,* which develop when snow and ice accumulate over a large area and build to a thickness of one or two miles. For example, even at the present time, the Greenland ice sheet occupies an area of 670,000 square miles and is about 10,000 feet thick at the center; the larger Antarctic ice sheet is about one and a half times as big as the United States and reaches a thickness of 2.5 miles. Spreading from the center, or *zone of accumulation,* a continental ice sheet flows outward in all directions, like pancake batter spooned onto a griddle, although the perimeter may be very uneven, depending on the topography of the land. At the beginning of the Pleistocene epoch (or Ice Age) in North America about one million years ago, when the world climate was somewhat cooler than at present, snow accumulated in Labrador and northwestern Canada, and from there the ice sheets spread radially until they merged and covered all of Canada and most of the United States north of New Jersey, Pennsylvania, and the Ohio and Missouri Rivers. At the same time, continental glaciers also spread from other, similar zones of accumulation in Scandinavia, Siberia, and Antarctica. In fact, in Europe the first Pleistocene glacier appears to have occurred about two million years ago.

Corresponding to the zone of accumulation at the center of the ice sheet is the *zone of wastage* at the perimeter. The wastage is caused by melting and evaporation (together called *ablation*) and by the *calving* of icebergs where the glacier meets the ocean. If the rate at which the glacier moves forward

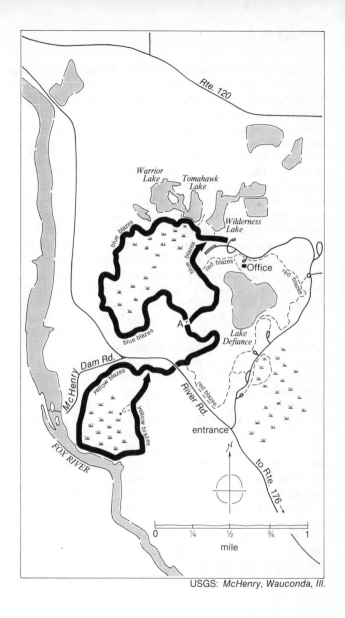

Warrior
Lake

Tomahawk
Lake

Wilderness
Lake

blue blazes

blue blazes

red blazes

■Office

red blazes

blue blazes

A ■

Lake
Defiance

McHenry Dam Rd.

yellow blazes

red blazes

River Rd.

yellow blazes

entrance

FOX RIVER

to Rte. 176

Rte. 120

N

0   ¼   ½   ¾   1
mile

USGS: *McHenry, Wauconda, Ill.*

181

is greater than the rate of wastage, then on balance the ice sheet advances. If the ice front melts as fast as the glacier moves, the perimeter is stationary. And if the ice sheet melts faster than it moves, the glacier recedes.

Glaciers act as huge earth scrapers and conveyor belts rolled into one. As it moves, the ice strips away the soil and grinds down the bedrock of the vast area over which the glacier advances. The immense weight of the ice even depresses the crust of the earth, so that the land surface beneath the glacier sinks (but later rises, or rebounds, after the ice melts). Boulders, rock fragments, sand, and a huge amount of finely pulverized rock called *rock flour* become imbedded in the glacier and constitute its *load,* which is carried forward by the ice sheet and deposited when the glacier melts. As boulders are dragged and scraped along the surface beneath the glacier, they sometimes leave scratches that can be traced for hundreds of miles across the bedrock (after the ice sheet melts, of course) and that show the direction from which the glacier advanced.

During the Pleistocene epoch, there were four distinct periods of continental glaciation in North America. The most recent ice sheet is termed the Wisconsinan glacier, but it reached as far south as central Illinois. The Wisconsinan glacier advanced about 70,000 years ago and retreated from the Chicago region only 12,500 years ago. The retreat was spasmodic; periods of steady withdrawal alternated with periods during which the ice front was stationary and even advanced again. In each case the earth materials carried by the glacier were deposited to create characteristic landforms. The most common assemblage of deposits is that of an *end moraine* fronted by an *outwash plain* and backed by a *ground moraine*.

An end moraine occurs where the ice front is stationary for a period. The glacier continues to flow foward, carrying its load of debris with it, but the rate of flow is more or less matched by the rate of wastage, so that the debris is dumped in a line along the ice front. The result is a range of irregular hills composed of unsorted clay, sand, rock fragments, and angular boulders that together are called *glacial till* or *boulder clay.* Such a ridge or hill complex may be many miles wide and scores of miles long, in which case some authorities term the end moraine a *morainic system.* The southern end of Lake Michigan is ringed by successive parallel end moraines. The irregular surface of the end moraines is described as *knob and kettle* topography, consisting of alternating hills and hollows. Many of the hollows are occupied by lakes, ponds, or marshes.

Sometimes *glaciofluvial deposits* occur where till has been reworked and sorted by running water. For example, mounds of layered glacial sand and well-washed gravel are called *kames;* they are associated with end moraines and are thought to be places where torrents of meltwater poured down the sloping ice front, washing away the clay and silt but leaving behind the heavier material. Also, crevasses that developed in the stagnant ice may have become filled with sand and gravel washed into them by meltwater; after the ice melted, the deposits were left as steep heaps or ridges.

In front of the end moraine — that is, in the direction toward which the ice advanced — is the *outwash plain.* After flowing swiftly down the front of the moraine, numerous meltwater streams that were loaded with sediments deposited *alluvial fans* or *outwash fans* where the streams reached more level terrain. Over time the alluvium spread and coalesced to form a continuous apron sloping slightly away from the end moraine. Because the energy of the meltwater dissipated as the streams fanned out, the deposits are graded; coarse gravel and sand were dropped close to the moraine, but the rock flour, which gives glacial streams their characteristic milky appearance, was carried much farther. In general, the outwash plain is nearly flat, but in front of an end moraine it may be pitted with *kettle holes* that once were filled with blocks of stagnant ice. The blocks became buried in the outwash, but after the ice finally melted, the debris with which the ice blocks were covered collapsed to form steep-sided holes. Again, these holes frequently are occupied by ponds and marshes.

In back of the end moraine — that is, on the side from which the ice advanced — is the *ground moraine*. The base of a glacier may become so overloaded with debris scoured from the land over which the ice sheet has advanced that some of this material drops out even as the glacier continues to move over it. When the glacier recedes, additional unsorted debris is left behind, so that a vast area is blanketed by till, producing a landscape of gently rolling upland and undrained or poorly-drained flats. *Erratics* — large boulders that have been moved by the ice far from their original locations — are visible here and there or are buried in the till. Also, low, elongated hills called *drumlins* may dot the landscape. Drumlins typically occur in areas underlain by bedrock that is relatively soft, like shale, and hence was easily ground into sticky clay. Gradually the ice flowed over these masses, adding still more earth and rock to them and molding them into their oval, streamlined shape. Drumlins, which may be more than 100 or 150 feet high and more than half a mile long, are common in Wisconsin. Yet another (though rare) feature of the ground moraine is a sinuous ridge of water-sorted sand and gravel that may extend for miles, usually in a course more or less parallel with the direction of the ice movement. Such a formation is called an *esker* and is thought to be deposited by a meltwater stream flowing through a tunnel beneath the ice or along the bottom of a large crack.

Although northeastern Illinois shows a remarkable series of end moraines, outwash plains, and ground moraines, each with its characteristic features, it is important to bear in mind that these landforms are not always distinct. Frequently they grade into each other and may even obscure one another. For example, where end moraines occur in close proximity, the outwash plain of one may overlie the ground moraine of another. Also, successive end moraines that in some places are far apart may in other areas merge because the glacier did not retreat at the same rate along the entire ice front. Nonetheless, as you take the walk described below (and also some of the other excur-

sions outlined in this book), you should have no trouble picking
out the more striking glacial features.

AUTOMOBILE: Moraine Hills State Park is located on the
Fox River northwest of Chicago and about 3 miles
downstream from McHenry. The entrance is on River Road
2.1 miles north of the intersection with Route 176.

From Chicago take Interstate 90 (Kennedy Expressway)
northwest toward O'Hare Airport and Rockford. As you
approach O'Hare, stay on I-90 as it becomes the
Northwest Tollway toward Rockford and Elgin. The
Northwest Tollway can also be reached via the Tri-State
Tollway east of O'Hare Airport.

Follow I-90 (the Northwest Tollway) about 8.4 miles
beyond the first toll plaza, then take the exit for Route 53
north toward Rolling Meadows. Follow Route 53 about 6
miles to the exit for Route 68 (Dundee Road). (Presently,
there is only one exit ramp at Route 68, but it a full
cloverleaf is ever built, take the westbound exit.) At the top
of the exit ramp, turn left (or, if a westbound exit has been
built, merge smoothly onto Route 68). Go 1 mile west on
Route 68, then turn right onto Route 12 (Rand Road). This
intersection can also be reached by following Route 68
west from the vicinity of Glencoe or east from
Carpentersville.

From the intersection of Route 68 (Dundee Road) and
Route 12 (Rand Road), follow Route 12 northwest 11.4
miles to the exit for Route 176 (Liberty Road). From the
bottom of the exit ramp, turn left and follow Route 176
west 3.4 miles, then turn right onto River Road. Follow
River Road 2.1 miles, then turn right into Moraine Hills
State Park. Follow the entrance road 2.7 miles to the
parking lot on the right for the Wilderness Lake area. If the
lot is full, park in one of the other nearby lots.

WALK: From the entrance to the parking lot for the

decayed plants. The result is extensive areas of marsh and a few bogs. As the process of filling-in continues, these areas eventually will become low, wet woods.

Bogs occupy approximately the midpoint along the line of succession by which open water is transformed into sodden land. Imagine a rock dropped at the center of a pond, so that little waves ripple outward toward the shore in concentric rings. Now picture this event in reverse, so that one after another the concentric ripples move from the shore and close in on the center. This shore-to-center motion is suggestive of the process by which, over a long period of time, concentric rings of distinctive plant communities start at the bank of a lake or pond and spread toward the center as the water is filled in.

In the first stage of transition, the water is ringed by submerged aquatic plants growing from the bottom around the perimeter of the pond. In the second stage, water lillies and other floating-leaved plants form a border along the shore, while the submerged aquatic plants have moved farther toward the center, contributing their remains to the accumulation of muck at the bottom of the pond. Next a thin, floating mat of leatherleaf (the main bog shrub) spreads from the shore.

Because of its vigorously branching habit of growth, leatherleaf forms a continuous tangle of vegetation in which separate plants cannot be distinguished. The floating carpet of leatherleaf may be supported in part by logs that have fallen into the pond or by rafts of fallen reeds, but for the most part bouyancy is provided by sphagnum moss growing among the densely intertwined branches of leatherleaf. The sphagnum floats because of gases trapped within the mossy mass. The moss also forms a moist carpet where the leatherleaf branches, as they spread out and sag to the surface of the bog under their own weight and the yearly burden of snow, become imbedded and sprout adventitious roots that further bind the mass together and establish a new locus of leatherleaf growth. As branches, leaves, and moss accumulate over the years, the mat of vegetation increases in weight and sinks lower in the water.

mile

Although the submerged leatherleaf and sphagnum moss die, the portion of the plant matrix that remains above the surface of the water continues to thrive and to replenish itself, so that the mat slowly thickens and eventually comes to rest at the bottom of the pond.

Long before the floating mat touches bottom, however, it forms a foundation for other shrubs and plants adapted to the unusual bog environment. One common bog shrub is poison sumac, which has compound leaves and off-white berries during the summer and fall. (To be on the safe side, do not handle any unfamiliar shrubs.) As soil begins to develop, trees appear in areas that once were open water but now are filled with muck and partially-decayed plant debris. Tamarack or American larch — a conifer that drops its needles in winter — often is found in bogs; tamarack roots are very shallow so as to avoid the soggy substrate and to support the tree in very unstable, wet soil.

Meanwhile, of course, aquatic plants and the floating mat of leatherleaf and sphagnum moss continue to close in on the center of the pond. As tamarack in turn advances toward the center, deciduous trees such as red maple, yellow birch, and serviceberry begin to take over near the shore. Eventually, forest will occupy the entire bog. But until it does, the bog may show a series of plant communities in concentric rings, with a small pond at the center like the bull's-eye of a target. This spot of open water is all that remains of what was once a much larger (though shallow) glacial lake.

Such, at any rate, is the idealized, textbook bog. You can judge for yourself the extent to which Volo Bog conforms to this model.

One characteristic of bogs is that they are singularly deficient in plant nutrients. The mat of leatherleaf and sphagnum moss tends to retain rainwater, which has a very low mineral content. The sodden layer of sphagnum also seals the underlying pond water off from the air, so that conditions low in oxygen develop. Decay of the vegetable debris below the surface of the water slows down, and so peat accumulates. The type of decay

VOLO BOG

that does occur under these anerobic bog conditions consumes
nitrogen — a major nutrient — and produces acid, which
makes absorption of water difficult for most plants. Acid is
also produced directly by the sphagnum, which has the property of absorbing bases and freeing acids. The fallen needles of
tamarack, which release tannic acid as they steep in the water
and decompose, adds to the acidity. The result is a hostile
environment for most plants. Those that survive show special
and sometimes bizarre adaptations. For example, the waxy, dry
leaves of leatherleaf reflect its need to retain water, even though
its roots are immersed in sodden moss. Pitcher plants and
sundew, which are common bog plants, obtain nitrogen and
other nutrients by trapping and digesting insects.

Although wetlands appear to be wastelands as far as human
activity is concerned, they lend valuable support to human
settlement, farming, and commerce. Marshes serve to replenish ground water that ultimately feeds wells for drinking,
agriculture, and industry. Wetlands are also settling and filter-
ing basins, collecting silt from upland erosion that otherwise
would choke streams. Wetlands are often called natural
sponges that absorb huge quantities of storm runoff, then release the water slowly over a period of weeks or months. In this
way they prevent or moderate floods and also keep streams
flowing throughout the year that otherwise would dry up after
each rainfall like a southwestern arroyo. In ways that are not
fully understood, wetlands also affect the levels of nearby
lakes, some of which have immense recreational value. And
apart from their direct value to humans, wetlands provide
habitat for many animal species.

The preservation of Volo Bog is the result of work by the
Illinois Chapter of The Nature Conservancy. The Nature Conservancy is a national organization that buys environmentally
unique or significant areas in order to preserve them in a
natural condition. In 1958 The Nature Conservancy purchased
47.5 acres at Volo Bog, and twelve years later transferred the
tract to the Illinois Department of Conservation, which has
since acquired more surrounding land.

AUTOMOBILE: Volo Bog is located northwest of Chicago, about 4 miles east of McHenry. The entrance is on Brandenburg Road 1.1 miles west of Route 12.

From Chicago take Interstate 90 (Kennedy Expressway) northwest toward O'Hare Airport and Rockford. As you approach O'Hare, stay on I-90 as it becomes the Northwest Tollway toward Rockford and Elgin. The Northwest Tollway can also be reached via the Tri-State Tollway east of O'Hare Airport.

Follow I-90 (the Northwest Tollway) about 8.4 miles beyond the first toll plaza, then take the exit for Route 53 north toward Rolling Meadows. Follow Route 53 about 6 miles to the exit for Route 68 (Dundee Road). (Presently, there is only one exit ramp at Route 68, but if a full cloverleaf is ever built, take the westbound exit.) At the top of the exit ramp, turn left (or, if a westbound exit has been built, merge smoothly onto Route 68). Go 1 mile west on Route 68, then turn right onto Route 12 (Rand Road). This intersection can also be reached by following Route 68 west from the vicinity of Glencoe or east from Carpentersville.

From the intersection of Route 68 (Dundee Road) and Route 12 (Rand Road), follow Route 12 northwest 18.6 miles, then turn left onto Brandenburg Road. Go 1.1 miles, then turn left into the parking lot for Volo Bog.

WALK: From the back-right corner of the parking lot, follow the path uphill to a barn and silo that now serve as the visitor center.

From the visitor center, follow the bog trail downhill past a path intersecting from the left. At the bottom of the slope, head straight out across the marsh on a boardwalk that leads to a small pond at the center of the bog. Continue around the boardwalk circuit back to the visitor center.

195

20

KETTLE MORAINE STATE FOREST
southern unit

Walking or ski touring — 2 to 9 miles (3.2 to 14.5 kilometers), depending on which of several trail circuits you follow. Still longer excursions are possible by combining trails on either side of Route H, as shown on the map. The trails climb, dip, and wind through a remarkable landscape of irregular hills and abrupt depressions. Dogs must be leashed. Open daily from 6:00 A.M. to 11:00 P.M. A user fee is charged. Managed by the Wisconsin Department of Natural Resources. Telephone (414) 594-2135.

THE BIZARRE LANDSCAPE of ridges, humps, and hollows explored by this walk is to the word *moraine,* what the Matterhorn is to the word *alp.* The Kettle Moraine is the quintessential moraine, the moraine at its fullest development. One geologist (W. C. Alden) has described the Kettle Moraine as the "master topographic feature of the whole series of glacial deposits in eastern Wisconsin. It was this which first attracted the attention of early explorers and led eventually to the refinement of glacial studies of the present day throughout this whole region." Indeed, the Kettle Moraine and the other outstanding examples of glacial landforms that are found in Wisconsin are the main reason that the most recent occurrence of continental glaciation is termed the Wisconsinan ice sheet, even though it also affected most of Canada and the entire northern tier of the United States east of the Rocky Mountains.

According to Thomas C. Chamberlin, a geologist who specialized in the study of glacial deposits and who served as president of the University of Wisconsin from 1887 to 1892, the Kettle Moraine is made up of a "series of rudely parallel ridges, that unite, interlock, separate, appear and disappear in an eccentric and intricate manner. . . . The component ridges are themselves exceedingly irregular in height and bredth, being often much broken and interrupted. The united effect of all the foregoing features is to give to the formation a strikingly irregular and complicated aspect." Taken altogether, the Kettle Moraine stretches 150 miles from the base of the Green Bay peninsula south-southwest to the vicinity of Palmyra. It varies in width from one to thirty miles, and the deposits of clay, sand, and boulders of which it is composed are as much as three hundred feet thick.

By far the most remarkable aspect of the moraine is the numerous pits or kettles for which the moraine is named. Some of these depressions have the shape of an inverted cone or bell; others are oval or irregularly shaped. In depth some are merely shallow saucers, but others are more than one hundred feet deep. Some are marshy at the bottom and others are occupied by ponds and even large lakes. The slope of the sides varies greatly, but in the deeper kettles, it often reaches an angle of 30 or 35 degrees — that is, about as steep as the earth material will lie. The pits range in diameter from a few hundred feet to thousands of yards, although those popularly recognized as "kettles" seldom exceed five hundred feet across. Referring to the kettles, one early geological investigator (Charles Whittlesey) wrote in 1860: "In travelling through such a region the explorer frequently finds them so near together, that he no sooner rises out of one than he is obliged immediately to descend into another, the diameter of which may not be more than twice or thrice its depth." It is these numerous crater-like hollows that make the Kettle Moraine such an intriguing place to walk. And the region is also characterized by countless rounded hills and knobs that might aptly be styled inverted kettles.

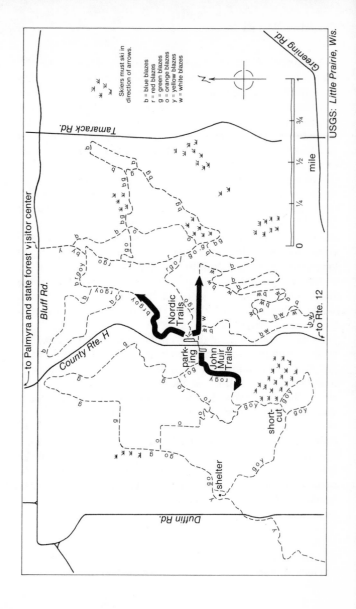

Greening Rd.

USGS: *Little Prairie, Wis.*

Tamarack Rd.

Skiers must ski in
direction of arrows.

b = blue blazes
r = red blazes
g = green blazes
o = orange blazes
y = yellow blazes
w = white blazes

N

0   ¼   ½   ¾   1
        mile

to Palmyra and state forest visitor center

Bluff Rd.

County Rte. H

Nordic Trails

parking

John Muir Trails

to Rte. 12

short-cut

shelter

Duffin Rd.

199

As discussed in prior chapters (see particularly Chapter 18), the kettles are not confined to the Kettle Moraine. Rather, they are typical of moraines and outwash plains. They were formed when huge blocks of stagnant ice became imbedded or even buried in the unconsolidated clay, sand, and cobbles deposited along the margin of the glacier. When the isolated blocks of ice melted, the surrounding earth slumped to form the kettles seen today.

Among geologists, the Kettle Moraine is known as the Kettle Interlobate Moraine, signifying that it was formed between two immense tongues of ice, one occupying the basin of Lake Michigan and the other the valley of Green Bay. Both lobes advanced primarily southward, but they also increased in width, so that the ice at the western edge of the Lake Michigan lobe actually moved toward the southwest, and the ice at the eastern margin of the Green Bay lobe advanced toward the southeast. As the two lobes of ice grew wider and even touched, the Kettle Interlobate Moraine was deposited in a long, narrow band between them.

At the southern end of the interlobate moraine, the morainic system splits in two. One branch heads west through Milton and then north through Madison and central Wisconsin, where it marks the outer limit of the Green Bay lobe. The other branch heads southwest past Lake Geneva and into Illinois, where it merges with the morainic systems that ring Lake Michigan. On a grand scale and in simplified outline, the configuration of end moraines resembles a nicely rounded cursive double-u (although the righthand u is longer and wider than the left). The Lake Michigan lobe occupied the u to the right, then Green Bay lobe the u to the left, and the Kettle Interlobate Moraine constitutes the vertical stroke between the two.

AUTOMOBILE: Kettle Moraine State Forest (southern unit) is located in Wisconsin about 20 miles north of Lake Geneva. The walks described here start at two parking

lots located on County Route H 4.6 miles south of
Palmyra.

From Chicago take Interstate 90 (Kennedy Expressway)
northwest toward O'Hare Airport and Rockford. As you
approach O'Hare, stay on I-90 as it becomes the
Northwest Tollway toward Rockford and Elgin. The
Northwest Tollway can also be reached via the Tri-State
Tollway east of O'Hare Airport.

Follow I-90 (the Northwest Tollway) about 8.4 miles
beyond the first toll plaza, then take the exit for Route 53
north toward Rolling Meadows. Follow Route 53 about 6
miles to the exit for Route 68 (Dundee Road). (Presently,
there is only one exit ramp at Route 68, but if a full
cloverleaf is ever built, take the westbound exit.) At the top
of the exit ramp, turn left (or, if a westbound exit has been
built, merge smoothly onto Route 68). Go 1 mile west on
Route 68, then turn right onto Route 12 (Rand Road). This
intersection can also be reached by following Route 68
west from the vicinity of Glencoe or east from
Carpentersville.

From the intersection of Route 68 (Dundee Road) and
Route 12 (Rand Road), follow Route 12 northwest slightly
more than 60 miles into Wisconsin and past exits for Lake
Geneva and Elkhorn. (Note also that Route 12 can be
reached northwest of Fox Lake by following Route 173
(Rosecrans Road) west from the Tri-State Tollway; in this
case, follow Route 12 northwest 27 miles.)

At an intersection where Route 12 turns left and Route
67 goes straight, turn left to continue west on Route 12.
Go 2 miles, then turn right onto County Route H. Follow
County Route H 1.5 miles north to the parking lots for the
Nordic hiking and skiing trails on the right and the John
Muir hiking and skiing trails on the left.

As signs at the parking lots explain, there is a user fee
for these areas. If there is a ranger at the parking lots, he
will collect your fee. Alternatively, collection boxes may be

installed at the parking lots. If a ranger is not present and there is no collection box, there are two ways to pay your fee. The first is to allow your car to be ticketed for the amount of the fee, then to mail the fee to the address on the ticket. The other way is to drive to the visitor center, where there are some interesting exhibits. The visitor center is reached by continuing north on County Route H for 4.6 miles to an intersection with Route 59 in the center of Palmyra. Go straight on Route 59 for 3.3 miles to the entrance to the visitor center on the right.

WALK: There are five trail circuits at the Nordic area and three trail circuits at the John Muir area. The different loops are marked with different color blazes. Typically, the trails start together (that is, congruent), then the shortest loop peels off to return to the parking lot; later the next shortest loop peels off, and so on. There is also the yellow-blazed Ice Age Trail, which stretches from one end of the state forest to the other, but follows portions of the trail loops at the Nordic and John Muir areas.* So before you start, examine the map board at each of the two parking lots and decide which trail circuit you want to follow.

For the Nordic area, start at the map board at the center of the east side of the parking lot. Turn left and follow the posts blazed with blue, red, green, orange, and yellow blazes into the woods and around whichever loop you choose. Or, if you want to take the white trail circuit, turn right from the map board, then turn left onto a fire road.

For the John Muir area, follow a mown swath across a meadow. At the trail posts near the edge of the woods, follow the red, green, orange, and yellow blazes toward the left and around whichever trail loop you choose.

---

*Actually, the Ice Age Trial stretches from Green Bay in the east to Minnesota in the west, but at present some segments are simply automobile roads. For information write to Ice Age Park and Trail Foundation of Wisconsin, Inc.; 780 North Water Street, Milwaukee, Wisconsin 53202.

BIBLIOGRAPHY

The numbers in parentheses at the end of the citations refer to the chapters in this book that are based on the cited material.

Black, Robert F., Ned K. Bleuer, Francis D. Hole, Norman P. Lasca, and Louis J. Maher. *Pleistocene Geology of Southern Wisconsin*. Madison: Geological and Natural History Survey, Information Circular Number 15, 1970. (20)

Borror, Donald J. *Common Bird Songs*. New York: Dover Publications, 1967. (6)

Brockman, C. Frank. *Trees of North America*. New York: Golden Press, 1968. (14)

Choate, Ernest A. *The Dictionary of American Bird Names*. Boston: Gambit, 1973. (17)

Collinson, Charles, Jerry Lineback, Paul B. DuMontelle, Dorothy C. Brown, Richard A. Davis, Jr., and Curtis E. Larsen. *Coastal Geology, Sedimentology, and Management — Chicago and the Northshore*. Illinois State Geological Survey, Guidebook Series 12, 1974. (1)

Cooper, Tom C., Editor. *Iowa's Natural Heritage*. DesMoines: Iowa Natural Heritage Foundation and the Iowa Academy of Sciences, 1982. (16)

Cowles, Henry Chandler. "The Ecological Relations of the

Vegetation of the Sand Dunes of Lake Michigan." *Botanical Gazette* 27, 1899. (8)

Daniel, Glenda, *Dune Country.* Athens, Ohio: Swallow Press, 1984. (8)

Farb, Peter. *The Land and Wildlife of North America.* New York: Time Incorporated, 1964. (16)

Franklin, Kay and Norma Schaeffer. *Duel for the Dunes.* Urbana: University of Illinois Press, 1983. (9)

Garrels, Robert M. *A Textbook of Geology.* New York: Harper, 1951. (4, 5, 18)

Gruson, Edward S. *Words for Birds.* New York: Quadrangle Books, 1972. (17)

Gurin, Joel. "Birds' Songs Are More Than Music." *Smithsonian,* Vol. 13, No. 4, pp. 118-127. (6)

Hester, Norman C. and Gordon S. Fraser. *Sedimentology of a Beach Ridge Complex and Its Significance in Land-Use Planning.* Urbana: Illinois State Geological Survey, Environmental Geology Notes, Number 63, 1973. (1)

Hill, John R. *The Indiana Dunes — Legacy of Sand.* Bloomington, Indiana: Department of Natural Resources, Geological Survey Special Report 8, 1974. (7, 10)

Johnson, James D. *Aurora "N" Elgin.* Wheaton: The Traction Orange Company, 1965. (15)

Larsen, Curtis E. *A Stratigraphic study of beach features of the southwestern shore of Lake Michigan: new evidence of Holocene lake level fluctuations.* Urbana: Illinois State Geological

Survey, Environmental Geology Notes, Number 112, 1985. (1, 7)

McComas, Murray R., John P. Kempton, and Kenneth C. Hinkley. *Geology, Soils, and Hydrology of Volo Bog and Vicinity, Lake County, Illinois*. Urbana: Illinois State Geological Survey, Environmental Geology Notes, Number 57, 1972. (19)

Morrison, Samuel Eliot. *The Oxford History of the American People*. New York: Oxford University Press, 1965. (11)

Pasquier, Roger F. *Watching Birds*. Boston: Houghton Mifflin, 1980. (6)

Peterson, Roger Tory. *A Field Guide to the Birds of Eastern and Central North America*. Boston: Houghton Mifflin, 1980. (6)

_____. *How to Know the Birds*. New York: Mentor Books, 1949. (6)

Petrides, George A. *A Field Guide to Trees and Shrubs*. Boston: Houghton Mifflin, 1958. (14)

Rathbun, Mary Yeater. *The Illinois and Michigan Canal* (draft). Illinois Department of Conservation, Division of Historic Sites, Office of Research and Publications, 1980. (11)

Robbins, Chandler S., Bertel Brun, and Herbert S. Zim. *Birds of North America*. New York: Golden Press, 1966. (6)

Smith, Ellen Thorne. Chicagoland Birds. Chicago: Field Museum of Natural History, 1972. (6)

Swan, J. M. A. and A. M. Gill. "The Origins, Spread, and

Consolidation of a Floating Bog in Harvard Pond, Petersham, Massachusetts. *Ecology,* Vol. 51, No. 5, 1970. (19)

Thompson, Richard A. *Around the Arboretum*. DuPage County Historical Society, 1981. (14)

Vierling, Philip E. *Starved Rock Trails*. Chicago: Illinois Country Outdoor Guides, 1978. (12)

Waldron, Larry. *The Indiana Dunes*. Eastern Acron Press, 1983. (8, 10)

Watts, Mary Theilgaard. *Reading the Landscape of America*. New York: Collier Books, 1975. (8, 19)

Willman, H. B. *Summary of the Geology of the Chicago Area*. Urbana: Illinois State Geological Survey, Circular 460, 1971. (7, 12)

ORDER FORM

If you do not want to tear out this page, simply send the necessary information to the address below.

Rambler Books
1430 Park Avenue
Baltimore, MD 21217

Please send me _____ copies of <u>Country Walks Near Chicago</u> at $8.95 apiece ($6.95 apiece if ordering five or more). My payment in the amount of _____ is enclosed. Price includes shipping and handling.

_____ Please send me a list and order form for your Country Walks books about cities other than Chicago.

Send books and/or information to (please print):

Name: _____

Address: _____

_____ Zip: _____

Expect two or three weeks for delivery of books.